COCKEYED HAPPY

COCKEYED HAPPY

Ernest Hemingway's Wyoming Summers with Pauline

Darla Worden

CHICAGO
REVIEW
PRESS

Copyright © 2021 by Darla Worden
All rights reserved
First hardcover edition published in 2021
First paperback edition published in 2023
Published by Chicago Review Press Incorporated
814 North Franklin Street
Chicago, Illinois 60610
ISBN 978-1-64160-898-5

The Library of Congress has cataloged the hardcover edition under the following
Control Number: 2021936736

The Letters of Ernest Hemingway (in the USA) © The Ernest Hemingway
Foundation and Society 2021
The Letters of Ernest Hemingway (outside the USA) © The Hemingway
Foreign Rights Trust 2021
Editorial matter © The Hemingway Letters Project, The Pennsylvania
State University 2021
The Cambridge edition of *The Letters of Ernest Hemingway, Volume 3 & 4*
(2015, 2017) by Ernest Hemingway. Copyright © Hemingway Foreign Rights Trust

Cover design: Jonathan Hahn
Cover photo: The Wyoming Room, Sheridan County Public Library System
Interior design: Nord Compo
Map design: Chris Erichsen

Printed in the United States of America

For Anna

CONTENTS

Part II: 1930

Part III: 1932

Part IV: 1936

Part V: 1938–1939

Epilogue: 1940

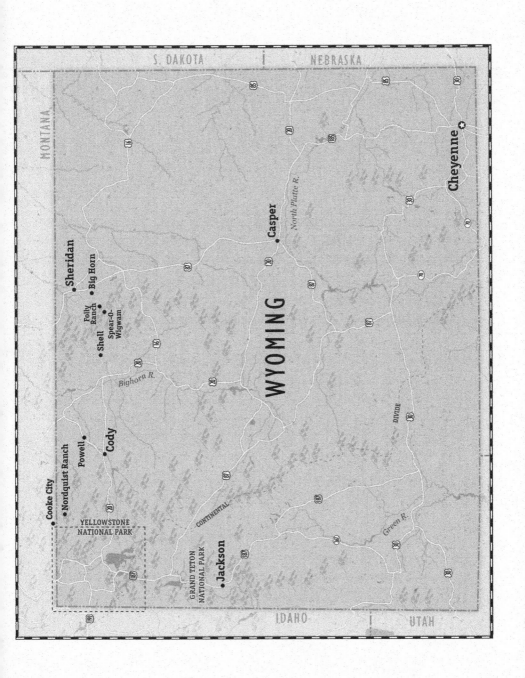

Part I

1928

What Ernest Loved About Pauline

Keen editorial eye
Her family became his family: Jinny, Mother Pfeiffer
Uncle Gus's support
Strong again
"Someone to feel swell with" after a day's work
The "feeling of us against the others"
Willing to join him on adventures
Believed in the "promotion of masculine society"
Vowed to always let him have his way
She could give him "little Pilar" in three years
Her throat never got sore like his
~~Spontaneous lovemaking~~*

---

* List compiled by the author from comments made by Ernest Hemingway
(EH) and Pauline Pfeiffer.

EXPLORERS COME WEST

HE'D NEVER BEEN OUT WEST BEFORE, but he'd heard it had some of the best fly-fishing in the world. As Ernest steered the yellow Model A toward the Bighorn Mountains, they reminded him of the Sierra de Guadarrama in Spain—the same color and shape but bigger. He missed Spain already. Because of Patrick's birth, he'd had to skip the San Fermin Festival in Pamplona this summer, and he swore he'd return next year. But for now, he and Bill Horne had driven three days from Kansas City to reach a dude ranch in Wyoming, where Ernest hoped to go fishing and finish his book.

Ernest recorded mileage each day—340, 380, 320. He liked to keep lists and record things, like how many fish he caught and game he shot. They had crossed a corner of Nebraska and come up the North Platte River into Wyoming—a changing landscape with hills like sand dunes, rocky outcroppings, buttes topped with scrubby ponderosa pine, and miles of sagebrush-speckled plains.

The entire country was baking in a heat wave, and forget about finding a cool drink to quench your thirst because of Prohibition—something that Ernest was having a hard time adjusting to after the Roaring Twenties in Paris, where liquor flowed freely. Finding liquor in America was like tracking game: you had to be stealthy. In Kansas City, though, he had connections, and he had brought four quarts of bootleg scotch for the trip.

Ernest had been planning to go out to Idaho, where you had to pack in on horseback, but Bill invited him to Folly Ranch and Ernest had accepted in spite of his feelings about dude ranches. If he could catch an enormous amount of trout without working too hard for them, he'd be happy. He also needed a respite from the awful heat and a quiet place to work.

It was July 30 when they turned onto a steep shale road that snaked up the mountainside, the coupe leaving a trail of red dust as it climbed. Ernest maneuvered the roadster around potholes, bumping over rocks and ruts, trying to stay away from the edge as Bill peered over the sheer drop-off where boulders the size of cars had tumbled thousands of feet to the valley floor.

"Look out, Ernie!" Bill yelled when Ernest came too near. The view was seductive—they could see the little towns of Sheridan and Big Horn in the valley below.

"Ernie, look out!" Bill shouted again.

"Do me a favor, Horney," Ernest said. "When you get out, just close the door." Bill didn't make a peep after that.

Ernest met Bill when they were in the *autoambulanzia** for the Red Cross in the Great War, on the Italian front, where they'd had to avoid more than potholes. He'd been nineteen, Bill, twenty-seven, and they'd traveled from New York to Paris, then to Milan and eventually Schio, Italy, where they were assigned to their posts. Bill had been there for him when Ernest was injured—227 shrapnel wounds in his leg—and they had been friends ever since.

The air became cooler as they gained altitude, and the breeze felt good. Kansas City had been too bloody hot, over ninety degrees each day. He hadn't been able to work in that heat, especially while worrying about Pauline, dangerously ill in the hospital. After the caesarean, she had to stay in the hospital for ten days due to gas distention, and at times Ernest had worried that it was the end for her. When she was finally out of the woods, he had taken her and their new son, Patrick Miller Hemingway, to stay with her family in Piggott, Arkansas, to recover while Ernest went fishing with Bill.

At a plateau, Ernest spotted a spring and pulled off the side of the road to fill up the car with water. The Ford was a wedding gift from Pauline's

---

* ambulance drivers.

rich uncle, Gus, who shipped it to them when they arrived in Key West, Florida, last April.* The company had only made fifty thousand of the model, and Uncle Gus wanted Pauline and Ernest to be one of the first to own one. Ernest had already logged seventy-six hundred miles in the car, beginning in Key West with his new father-in-law, Paul Pfeiffer, and driving together to the Pfeiffer home in Piggott. Pauline, who was then eight months pregnant, took the train. Riding for five days with someone you have only just met, in dreadful heat, on gravel roads, stopping at night to sleep in "tourist cabins," was a sure way to get to know a person.

And now driving with "Horney," someone he had not seen in seven years, was an opportunity to catch up—so much had happened. After Ernest married Hadley Richardson in 1921, they had moved to Paris. He had lived there until this spring, when he and Pauline had returned to the United States so their baby could be born here. He'd seen Bill just a few times on brief visits from Paris to the Hemingway family home in Oak Park, outside Chicago, where Bill lived. Now that Ernest was back, maybe he would see Bill more often. This trip gave them a chance to reminisce about their time in the war together; perhaps some of those stories would make their way into his new novel.

His first novel, *The Sun Also Rises*, had been published two years earlier while he was in Paris. He'd written about men who returned to Paris after the Great War—Gertrude Stein had called them "The Lost Generation"—drifters without purpose after what they had seen in the war. His new book took place in Italy, where Ernest had spent months recuperating in a Milan hospital after his injuries and had fallen in love with his nurse, Agnes von Kurowsky. His leg eventually healed, but his heart had been broken on receiving a letter from Agnes after he returned home, saying she was dumping him to marry a duke.

That was ten years ago, but he could still conjure those feelings— feelings he was putting into the story of a soldier falling in love with his nurse in Italy. He was on page 486, with a third still left to write, and he hoped to finish the "bloody book" in the solitude of Wyoming before Pauline joined him in a few weeks.

---

* They were married May 10, 1927.

At the spring, the men stretched their legs. Ernest was six feet tall, and Bill was even taller. The alpine meadows around them exploded with Indian paintbrush, lupine, and black-eyed Susans, and in the distance, they spotted a mountain range with a tall, snowcapped peak despite the summer heat. Bill said he felt "just as much explorers as Columbus was in the *Santa Maria*." Ernest welcomed the chance to discover this new place with the "Horned article" or "Article" for short—Ernest affectionately gave friends, family, even himself nicknames. Wyoming was the blank page just waiting for him to put his mark on it. To write, he needed something new: new lands, new experiences, and new people.

That's how *The Sun Also Rises* had come to him. After attending the bullfights in Pamplona with his friends, he'd been on fire. He had sat down at his typewriter, and ten weeks later had written a bestselling novel that was based on his experience. Critics called it a new style that combined journalistic reporting and real people with fiction techniques. It was thrilling to have written a book like that at age twenty-six, a book that rocked the literary world, even if many of those friends no longer spoke to him.

Back in the car, the road was so narrow in places that any cars headed downhill needed to yield to cars going uphill by allowing them to pass. Luckily, there weren't many cars coming down—mostly just cattle grazing in the mountain meadows and crossing the road when they felt like it.

Ernest steered onto a road that looked like a cattle trail and stopped at the ranch gate, where Eleanor Donnelley, their hostess, stood waiting to greet them, along with a surprise: fifteen of her friends from Bryn Mawr.

Shit, Ernest thought, so much for working.

STRENGTH
IN THE AFTERNOON

PAULINE WAS RESTING on the sofa of her parents' home in Piggott, writing Ernest a letter. Her mother would not allow her to use the typewriter upstairs, so she was forced to write the letter by hand. "Mother is a dragon about the steps," she wrote. The doctor had been clear after Patrick's birth: no stairs, no lifting, and no more children for three years unless she wanted to be an invalid or a corpse. Even though Ernest had hoped for a daughter they would name Pilar, he had seemed content with another son: Patrick Miller Hemingway, born June 28, 1928.

John Hadley Nicanor Hemingway, or "Bumby," was nearly five years old and lived with his mother, Hadley, in Paris. Now the father of two boys, Ernest might joke to his friends that fatherhood was overrated, and he couldn't understand why anyone would want to be a father. He warned them that babies bellow, and they can drive you crazy. But truth was, Ernest was a proud papa, bragging about Patrick's size and health and how he would teach Patrick to hunt quail one day.

Pauline had known Ernest would get restless while she recovered in Piggott with its unbearable heat, and he couldn't concentrate when a baby was crying, so she supported the idea of his Wyoming fishing trip with Bill. She recognized Ernest's need for male companionship—the "promotion of masculine society," she called it. They had barely unpacked their bags in Key West last spring when John Dos Passos, Waldo Peirce, and Henry "Mike" Strater arrived and stayed for nearly a month. She didn't object—despite being seven months pregnant—knowing how Ernest loved to discover new places and to share them with friends.

He hadn't been the first in his group to discover Key West; "Dos" was. They met in Paris and realized that their paths might have crossed during the Italian ambulance service. Dos—a well-known traveler and journalist—told Ernest about a trip he'd taken through Florida and about the magic of Key West. Ernest had wanted to see it for himself, so that's where he and Pauline stayed upon arriving from Paris. As much as they both fell in love with Key West, there was no way Pauline wanted to deliver her first child there. Instead, she looked for good obstetrical hospitals and chose one in Kansas City.

The Pfeiffer home in Piggott, Arkansas, had ample room for Pauline and Patrick to stay while mother and baby recovered. After all, her father had purchased it from the town's master builder, who had created it for his own family that included twenty-three children. The Pfeiffers had moved there from St. Louis, Missouri, after Pauline's high school graduation; her parents had wanted her to be able to graduate with her friends before relocating to their new home.

The two-story white Colonial Revival farmhouse in Piggott had five bedrooms, a music room, pressed tin ceilings, and glass-paneled doors. Situated on the edge of town, it was still just eight blocks from the town square across the street from the school. Paul Pfeiffer had deemed the home perfect for his family, which included Pauline, then seventeen and heading to college, and her younger siblings—Karl, entering seventh grade; sister Virginia, "Jinny," beginning fifth grade; and Max, starting kindergarten. Paul had made a generous offer to the builder, and the Pfeiffers moved in.

Because the closest Catholic church was thirty miles away and Mary Pfeiffer was a devout Catholic, Paul converted the music room into a chapel for her. Two years before Pauline returned to the house with infant Patrick, she had spent many hours in that chapel praying to Saint Joseph during the one-hundred-day ultimatum Hadley had given Ernest and Pauline when she discovered their affair.

Pauline had been living with Jinny in Paris in the spring of 1925 when they'd met Ernest and Hadley at Kitty Cannell's apartment near the Eiffel Tower. Kitty, the fashion editor for the *New York Times*, had invited the Pfeiffer sisters to an afternoon tea for Hadley. Kitty thought Pauline and Hadley would be fast friends because they had so much in common—they'd grown up in St. Louis and shared a friend, Katy Smith.

Hadley had met Katy at parochial school in St. Louis, and Pauline knew Katy from the University of Missouri Journalism School. She and Katy were in the first graduating class of journalists at a school that was the first of its kind in the country.

In another coincidence, Ernest knew Katy and her two brothers, Bill and Y. K., from childhood summers in Michigan—the Hemingway and Smith families both had retreats there. The Smith siblings were some of Ernest's closest friends, and he'd once had a crush on Katy.

At the tea, the ladies had been getting acquainted as Pauline told stories about her job in Paris at *Vogue*, where she was an editor. She described her boss, Main Bocher, as "ambrosial"—a popular superlative of the era. She and Jinny enjoyed the fast-paced, witty repartee of the times, using slang with ease.

When Ernest came in sweaty and disheveled from boxing with Kitty's lover Harold Loeb at a local gym, Pauline thought he seemed like a boring oaf. Jinny was the one who found Ernest fascinating. The two of them ended up sitting alone in the kitchen, chatting away about bicycle racing or some other sport. Seven years older than Jinny, Pauline had the role of looking out for her little sister, and she later lectured Jinny on the impropriety of it all. They were there to support Hadley, who didn't have many friends in Paris, not to talk with her husband alone in the kitchen. Pauline could not have imagined at that afternoon tea what the future would have in store for her.

Ernest and Jinny had become close friends after that day at Kitty's, sometimes meeting each other for dinner or drinks at a Left Bank café, and they still were. Not that Pauline minded. She was happy her sister and husband got along so well—Jinny had helped smooth a path with the Pfeiffer family when Pauline had worried about introducing Ernest to her parents, afraid what they would think when they learned he was a married man. Jinny emphasized to her parents how much Pauline loved

Ernest, and they had accepted him into the family despite the circumstances, partly due to her support and approval.

In the fall of 1925, Jinny was undecided about her future plans and returned to Piggott. Alone in Paris, Pauline had begun stopping by the Hemingways' apartment above a sawmill on her way home from the *Vogue* office to visit Hadley, who had become her friend. Hadley was often exhausted after taking care of Bumby all day, so she went to bed early, leaving Pauline and Ernest alone to discuss something he'd written. At age thirty, Pauline was between Ernest, twenty-six, and Hadley, thirty-four, in age, and she found herself in the middle of this friendship, feeling equally comfortable with Ernest and Hadley.

By then, her feelings for Ernest had changed. She no longer thought of him as that boring oaf she'd met at Kitty's apartment. He was so handsome, with dark hair and dark eyes that studied you as you spoke, really listening. Other than her brief engagement to her cousin Matthew Herold, which had ended after she moved to Paris, she was inexperienced around men and unprepared to resist Ernest's charms even if he was married to her friend.

———————

After Hadley had confronted Ernest about his affair with Pauline and saw that he wasn't willing to end it, she gave Ernest and Pauline an ultimatum: stay apart for one hundred days. If they still wanted to be together after that time, Hadley would give Ernest a divorce. Hadley had bet that when the two spent time apart, the flame between them would die.

While Ernest stayed in Paris at Gerald Murphy's studio, Pauline went home to Piggott to serve out the sentence. She had plenty of time to think about their actions and admitted they had overlooked Hadley's feelings. Pauline told Ernest that she feared while they were crazy in love with each other, Hadley "had been locked out."

Pauline had written Hadley to apologize and say that she didn't want Hadley to move forward with the divorce until she was certain that was what she wanted. Pauline cared for Hadley and didn't blame Hadley if she didn't trust her.

One day Ernest stopped by Hadley's Paris apartment to talk to her about their situation, and when she saw Ernest so emotionally distraught, she took pity on him and decided to call off her hundred-day separation. Ernest could have his divorce. Pauline had been "cockeyed happy" when she received the news in Piggott; her prayers to Saint Joseph had been answered.

Now that some time had passed, some of their relationship with Hadley had been repaired through Pauline's affection for Bumby. She'd been in his life since he was a toddler, loving him like her own child. Hadley had once written to Ernest, "Pauline has sent splendid letters about everything a mother and ex-wife wants to know. I am most grateful."

———————

The doctor had ordered Pauline to rest, so it was no wonder her mother was forcing her to strictly follow the rules as she focused on regaining her strength on the sofa in Piggott. "I'm not allowed to do anything," she complained to Ernest. "But I'm getting very strong, and soon there will be a big fight, and then I can do all the things I want." What she wanted was to be with him in Wyoming. "With you away, it seems as though I am just a mother, which is certainly not very gripping," she wrote. "But in three weeks I'll begin to get ready to go to Wyoming, where I shall be just a wife."

Patrick was faring well, surrounded by a household of women who doted on him—Pauline's mother, Mary; sister Jinny; and beloved housekeeper, Lillie—so Pauline was confident that he would be perfectly fine when she was away. In the hospital she'd quickly weaned him to a bottle, preparing the way for others to help with feedings. She had discovered that to keep Patrick pacified, increasing his formula did the trick. "We have a little slogan to keep Patrick a good boy," she wrote to Ernest. "It is Raise The Formula."

Being Mrs. Ernest Hemingway was Pauline's great joy; she believed that she and Ernest were two halves of the same person, and they were meant to be together. Even their birthdays—Ernest's on July 21 and

Pauline's on July 22, one day apart—were a meaningful coincidence. She willingly gave up her career at *Vogue* and her Paris world for him, exchanging cocktails at the Ritz and couture dresses for bootleg whiskey and maternity clothes and a life that revolved around Ernest's hobbies and needs. Giving birth to Patrick connected Pauline to Ernest in the same way that Hadley was—as mother to Ernest's child, Pauline would always have a special role in Ernest's life.

She knew how he could be, though; women seemed to gravitate to him, and he didn't like to be alone. But he was fishing in the Wyoming wilderness, so no need to worry about him finding company there.

FIFTEEN GIRLS

It wasn't that Ernest didn't like girls, he did—but that's what had gotten him in a jam with Hadley. After they'd met Pauline at Kitty's tea and she'd started stopping by their apartment, he realized she was a damned good editor and she admired him. Then one night when he was walking her to the corner, he realized he'd fallen in love and his troubles began.*

It was a curse, loving two women, and for a while he felt "shot all to hell inside." At first he'd thought it could just go on with Hadley as his wife and Pauline as his girl, but neither would settle for that arrangement. Pauline was a strict Catholic who insisted on being his wife, not his mistress, and he'd been forced to choose. There was no way he could give up the new, exciting love with Pauline, although he'd felt terrible about Hadley. He had written a letter telling her, "—and I think perhaps the luckiest thing Bumby will ever have is to have you for a mother . . . and I pray God always that he will make up to you the very great hurt that I have done you—who are the best and truest and loveliest person that I have ever known."

In the divorce he'd given Hadley every penny that he would ever make from *The Sun Also Rises*—he wanted to be certain she and Bumby

---

* In an unpublished sketch written by Hemingway in the 1920s (Item 648a, Ernest Hemingway Collection, John F. Kennedy Presidential Library and Museum, published in the *Hemingway Review*, Spring 1990), he wrote: "He had been married for five years and he'd never gone with another woman and suddenly he found himself in love with her."

13

would be taken care of—and it had worked out wonderfully. The book had sold well and was still selling; two Broadway producers had even contacted him about possibly adapting it for the stage, which would mean more money for Hadley and Bumby.

It hadn't taken long for Hadley to forgive him. She invited Ernest to come and see Bumby as much as he wished, and she'd forgiven Pauline to a degree since she would be in Bumby's life. When Hadley received Ernest's cable about Patrick's difficult birth, she wrote, "Give Pauline my love and Bumby's and heartiest congratulations on the size & sex & I imagine the attractiveness of her son and her own recovering from what I am sure must have been a hideous time." Hadley even enclosed a check to help with expenses.

In Paris, when Bumby was an infant, Ernest had walked down the street to the Closerie des Lilas to escape the "squalation" stage, as he called it, and sit in a booth with the light streaming over his shoulder as he wrote a story called "Big Two-Hearted River" about a young man named Nick Adams and a trout stream. This time, instead of a French café, he'd find solace in a remote Wyoming ranch and an actual trout stream.

Bill had told Ernest that Folly Ranch was a dude operation, and Ernest had still wanted to come despite his feelings about them. Popular among wealthy East Coast families, dude ranches sprang up in the 1920s as a way for ranchers to supplement income from cattle operations. Although he agreed to the visit, Ernest preferred spending time with the ranch hands and wranglers, the real people who lived and worked on the land, rather than dudes who came from the pages of the Social Register. This area in Wyoming was an incubator of dude ranch operations. Along Red Grade Road alone there were three—Teepee, Spear-O-Wigwam, and Folly—with several more in the valley below.

Eleanor Donnelley, of Chicago's R. R. Donnelley publishing family, had been a guest at Teepee Ranch when she fell in love with the Bighorn Mountains and borrowed money to buy land along Teepee's southern border. Her father paid off her debt, which she had said was "pure folly," and her Folly Ranch got its name. She invited many of her cousins, who attended Yale and Bryn Mawr (where Hadley had briefly attended university before dropping out due to health issues), to help her on the ranch each summer during their college breaks.

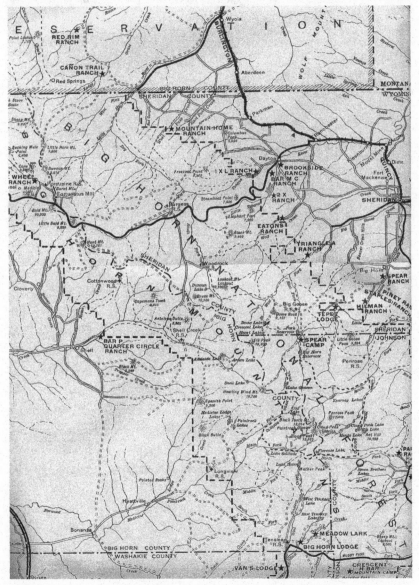

The Sheridan area was a popular location for dude ranches with an East coast clientele. *The Wyoming Room, Sheridan County Public Library System*

Folly Ranch was a small dude ranch operation, and most of its guests were friends and family of Eleanor Donnelley. *The Wyoming Room, Sheridan County Public Library System*

Folly Ranch was a typical "dude" setup, with guests staying in rustic log cabins, taking meals together family style in a main lodge, and participating in group activities like fishing, hiking, horseback riding, swimming in cold mountain lakes, and pack trips. Despite Ernest's misgivings about dude ranch life, Bill thought it was heaven, maybe in part because of the women, who were still mostly single, a few divorced, and "all very attractive."

Evenings were spent with the other guests, playing bridge and charades and singing around the piano. Ernest entertained the group with stories about Dorothy Parker and F. Scott Fitzgerald, and then digressed into a story about a bullfight, with his hands doing much of the talking as he acted out "both the matador and the bull."

With his sights on future fishing, Ernest had been studying a map of Wyoming and Montana on the wall, and he pointed out a little stream along Yellowstone Park's eastern border in northern Wyoming to Bill. It dropped down south through wilderness, then turned north to the Yellowstone River, hundreds of miles and several mountain ranges away from Folly.

Ernest and Bill Horne (back row, second from right, Ernest Hemingway; right, Bill Horne) sit with the Folly girls after swimming, 1928. *The Wyoming Room, Sheridan County Public Library System*

"Horney," Ernest said, "that's the place. Someday you and I'll go there and slaughter em!"

On his first morning on the ranch, Ernest rose early and worked, writing four pages before joining Bill to explore the wilderness. Folly, nestled into a private valley on four hundred acres with its own lake and a stream passing through, miles from the nearest town, seemed fine enough as Ernest and Bill tromped through the lightly timbered pine forests and open grassy meadows, fishing gear in tow.

Ernest's father, Clarence, an obstetrician, had taught Ernest and his five siblings to appreciate nature and the natural world. They had spent summers at their family retreat on Walloon Lake near Petoskey, Michigan, where Clarence taught them life skills like making a fire, identifying plants and animals, and shooting a gun. He told them to respect nature, including never killing anything unless you were going to eat it—a lesson that stuck with Ernest, who released fish that he didn't plan to consume. His first day at Folly, he caught twelve fish and recorded it in his fishing log.

Ernest with his rod and fishing creel in the Bighorns, 1928. *Ernest Hemingway Collection, John F. Kennedy Presidential Library and Museum, Boston*

On the second day, one of the Bryn Mawr girls took Ernest and Bill fishing on the east fork of Big Goose Creek, and the men discovered a nice stream called Cross Creek, but Ernest only caught two fish. On the third day, he set out alone, fished by himself, and caught thirty fish, the limit: twenty-six were eastern brook trout, and four were rainbows.

When he returned from his solo fishing day, the ranch was buzzing with preparations for Eleanor's annual party. Each August, she hosted two hundred couples who braved the mountain road, some by car, some by horse, to attend the social event of the season. Her famous dance and supper party was followed by a massive bonfire with wood stacked in the shape of a large teepee. The Bryn Mawr girls and Eleanor's wranglers and ranch hands were baking cakes, making punch, arranging flowers, building the dance floor, and stacking wood for the bonfire.

Guests began arriving at 7:00 PM, and couples soon crowded the floor, Ernest and Bill and the Bryn Mawr girls among them, dancing to

Wood stacked in the shape of a teepee for a bonfire at Eleanor Donnelley's
annual party, 1928. *The Wyoming Room, Sheridan County Public Library System*

Lyle Corey's orchestra—square dances, waltzes, and two-steps—until a
brief rainstorm paused the music. The dance floor was promptly dried
and the party continued.

At midnight, a supper of sandwiches, cake, ice cream, and coffee was
served, followed by the giant bonfire—its striking and somewhat frightening
silhouette against the dark night a spectacle that left some guests speechless
and produced so much heat, guests had to step back from the roaring flames.
Eventually, the fire died and couples returned to dancing under the stars.
Eleanor and friends enjoyed a 4:00 AM breakfast, then finally went to bed.

The late-night revelry was too much for Ernest. At 6:00 AM he packed
his car and left without saying goodbye, desperate to find a quiet writing space. Bill would understand; he'd always supported Ernest and his
writing—and besides, he'd have the Folly Ranch girls to entertain him.

The bonfire created a frightening silhouette and produced so much heat that guests had to stand back, 1928. *The Wyoming Room, Sheridan County Public Library System*

WYOMING WINE

SHERIDAN, LOCATED TWENTY MILES FROM FOLLY, was a charming town built by railroad and coal money. Stately Victorian homes sat upon wide, tree-lined boulevards, and it boasted two movie theaters and a Carnegie library for local literature lovers. The Sheridan Inn, a fine old hotel where Buffalo Bill Cody once auditioned acts for his Wild West Show, with its many-gabled roof and wide veranda, was conveniently located across the street from the train depot and walking distance to the downtown commercial district. Ernest signed the guest register the morning of August 3.

During the next week, Ernest produced nearly forty pages in his six-foot-by-nine-foot room, taking breaks by playing poker at the Mint Bar on Main Street. There, he met Howard Vickery, a local newspaper editor who offered to introduce Ernest to the local bootleggers, a nice French couple who sold wine and beer from their home on the edge of town. It wasn't always easy to find good booze during Prohibition, especially with the scar on his forehead that some people viewed with suspicion. Having a local connection made a difference.

He had gotten the scar in Paris the previous March after he and Pauline had been out to dinner with their friends Archibald and Ada MacLeish. "Archie" was a Yale-educated poet and his wife Ada, a concert singer living in Paris. In the night, Ernest had gone into the bathroom and, in the dark, yanked down a pull to a skylight instead of the toilet chain, sending the skylight crashing down on his head, slicing his face. Pauline called Archie for help, and they transported Ernest to the hospital for stitches that resulted in the large scar. He was getting used to it, but it gave him a rakish appearance, and

The Sheridan Inn in 1928, where Ernest worked on *A Farewell to Arms*.
The Wyoming Room, Sheridan County Public Library System

nobody in Key West believed he was a writer. His publisher, Charles Scribner's Sons, had removed the scar from a recently taken publicity photo for his upcoming novel.

———————

The valley was baking as Ernest drove down a dusty road north of town, to a row of small wooden houses away from the grand homes that lined Loucks Street. Sheridan didn't benefit from the cool mountain breezes felt at Folly Ranch. It was flatland, surrounded by yellow grain fields, green alfalfa, and sugar beet crops—and August was often the hottest month of the year.

Ernest pulled up in front of a modest home and knocked on the door.* A plump old woman with white hair answered and led him to

———————

* This chapter is based on EH correspondence and details found in "Wine of Wyoming," the short story about the French bootleggers in Sheridan he published in 1930.

a table on the back porch, bringing him a cold beer. A car pulled up and stopped, and two men walked toward the house. Ernest hid the beer under the table, not wanting to cause any trouble in case these men were agents. When the woman told them she didn't have any beer, they left.

The French bootlegger and his neighbor worked at the coal mine but relied on the extra money from their bootlegging operation to make a living. Ernest paid four dollars a gallon for wine and one dollar a gallon for beer, and he sat on the vine-shaded porch drinking the cold brew that tasted as good as the beer he had drunk at Brasserie Lipp in Paris.

He admired the snow-covered peak in the distance, and talked with the woman when she came back to the porch. When she learned Ernest was eating his meals at the hotel restaurant, she didn't approve—the food was no good there; he should eat with them. That evening, Ernest returned for dinner, talking with the couple in a combination of French and English.* They were a nice family just trying to make a living in this strange, dry country. Ernest learned the husband and their neighbor had been arrested twice on liquor charges, earlier in the year, paying a considerable amount in fines.

The wife was a good cook, serving chicken, fried potatoes, salad, corn, and cucumbers—and the husband brought out some of his new wine, "light and tasting of grapes." After dinner the discussion turned to religion; they were Catholics, and Ernest told them that he and his wife were, too. Ernest said that Pauline would love to meet them when she visited, and he promised to stop by.

Ernest didn't share with the French couple the story about when he felt he had really become a Catholic. It was after he and Pauline were married. He'd never had problems making love before and he didn't know why it was happening, so he made the rounds to doctors and even to a mystic who suggested he drink calf's blood every day. Finally,

---

* In a newspaper article appearing in the *Billings Gazette*, October 18, 1970, the French bootlegger couple was identified as the Moncinis. Their family challenged the article saying that the Moncini couple was misidentified, and that the neighbors named Pichot were probably the bootleggers Hemingway wrote about.

Pauline suggested that he go to a cathedral and pray. When he returned he found Pauline in bed, and they "never had any trouble again." Ernest missed Pauline terribly and was looking forward to the day she would arrive.

THEY GOT IT WRONG

THE *SHERIDAN JOURNAL* WROTE about Eleanor's annual party: "Among Miss Donnelley's guests is Ernest Hemingway, well known author who among recent years, has spent much of his time abroad. Mr. Hemingway who is an ardent and efficient fisherman, has written many well-received novels, his latest success, *Men Without Women*, now meeting with tremendous approval throughout the east."

Since the success of his novel *The Sun Also Rises*, Ernest had become fairly "well known" in the US press, as the article stated, which was sometimes good (he always enjoyed positive reviews of his work, and it helped sell books) and sometimes extremely annoying (when they got things wrong or pried into his personal business). When Ernest and Hadley were breaking up, he hadn't told his conservative Oak Park parents out of shame and fear of what they would say, but the newspapers had done the job for him.

His father wrote to him, asking if the rumors of his breakup were true, and asked him to "please write to me so I can deny the awful rumors." It took him several months after receiving the letter to fess up that indeed he and Hadley had separated, but still he denied his involvement with Pauline. He tried to minimalize his parents' concerns, saying Bumby and Hadley were doing well and they were the best of friends—and Ernest urged his parents to show him a little loyalty and not believe everything they hear.

Here in the *Sheridan Journal* was another instance of the paper having it all wrong: he'd only written *two* novels, *The Torrents of Spring* and *The Sun Also Rises*—not "many" as the paper stated. The novel had been successful, and his experience had been almost as one *New York Times* critic described: Ernest "wrote a book and woke up to find himself famous." The critic, Percy Hutchison, wrote, "Seldom has a book received such instantaneous recognition or been greeted with greater enthusiasm," despite the grumblings from some readers that it was disgusting. Even Ernest's own mother had called it "one of the filthiest books of the year." His dad, who had also been disappointed, was a little more tactful when he said he wished his son would use his wonderful ability in the future on a different subject.

His most recent book, *Men Without Women,* was not a novel as the *Sheridan Journal* had reported, but a collection of short stories published on October 14, 1927, while he was still in Paris. The jury was still out on whether it was indeed a success. His editor, Maxwell Perkins, said it was selling well, but some critics were not impressed, finding Ernest's subjects "lacking." The *New York Times Book Review*, however, called him a "master in a new manner of the short story form. . . . His style is his own."

Ernest loved the praise but couldn't stand criticism: What did critics know? He was proud of the stories in *Men Without Women*, especially one called "Fifty Grand," a damn good story about Jack Brennan, an aging boxing champ, during his last fight with Jim Walcott. The *Atlantic Monthly* had published "Fifty Grand" the previous year—the first national magazine to publish his short fiction after years of Ernest sending out stories and receiving rejections. More proof that these stories were good: "The Killers" appeared in Edward J. O'Brien's *The Best Short Stories of 1927.*

It irked him that he hadn't seen much recent advertising by Scribner's for *Men Without Women.* When Ernest asked Mr. Perkins about it, he responded that Scribner's had "eased off" advertising because business at Scribner's had been slow and it was a presidential year. Still, Ernest had seen a lot of advertising for Thornton Wilder's *The Bridge of San Luis Rey,* and it seemed like Scribner's had promoted *Men Without Women* at the first of the year, then dropped all marketing. Ernest was frustrated that it appeared other writers were "getting rich while he was making less than a newspaper correspondent."

He was supporting two families—Hadley and Bumby in Paris, and now Pauline and Patrick—and money was always on his mind despite Pauline's family wealth. He wasn't killing pigeons in Luxembourg Gardens for dinner anymore,* but there never seemed to be enough money. He hadn't sold a single story this year because he needed all his creative juice to go into his new book and he was nearly broke.

In January he had been working on a father-and-son novel when a new idea about the war, which had started out like a short story, continued to grow. In March, the skylight accident—the blood and stitches—brought back memories of the trenches and the fighting. Ernest had set aside the father-and-son story, twenty-two chapters, to pour his energy into the short story that had turned into a novel. He once told F. Scott Fitzgerald that in fiction, "war was the best subject of all, offering maximum material combined with maximum action." And now as he approached the story's ending, he needed a quiet space to finish the book—and the Sheridan Inn had not been the tranquil place he'd thought it would be. Guests visited each other in their rooms at all hours, talking in the halls, making a racket. Across the street, trains rattled through day and night, blowing their whistles. After four days in town he checked out, this time moving to an empty ranch at the base of the Bighorn Mountains also owned by Eleanor Donnelley, called Lower Folly.

---

* There are stories that he was so poor in Paris he once killed a pigeon in the Luxembourg Gardens for dinner.

A CLEAN,
WELL-LIGHTED RANCH

ON AUGUST 8, just outside the little town of Big Horn at the foot of Red Grade Road, Ernest pulled into an empty ranch without a dude in sight. The U-shaped house surrounded a swimming pool, built in a style that could have been found in a Chicago suburb, except it was built with logs.

Built by Chicago architect Stanley Anderson, the ranch house called Lower Folly was built with logs in a suburban architectural style.
The Wyoming Room, Sheridan County Public Library System

He quickly settled into his peaceful new surroundings and wrote—finishing seventeen and one-half pages his first day—a total of 2,550 words. Ernest often calculated his word production with ciphering in the margin of his notebooks or manuscripts, giving him satisfaction that he was moving toward the finish.

In celebration of a good day's work, he ate and drank too much with the ranch guys that night. The next morning, Ernest suffered from "gastric remorse,"* so he wrote letters instead of working on his novel. Though he loved to receive letters, he didn't write many when he was working on a book—he needed all his writing energy to go into his work. When the pain of a hangover impeded his creativity, however, he liked to write letters so he could feel like he had still accomplished something.

He wrote to Waldo Peirce, his painter friend from Paris** now living in Maine, describing Wyoming and how it reminded him of Spain. Waldo had joined him in Pamplona the previous year, instead of Pauline, because the Spanish people were against divorce and Ernest felt it was too soon to introduce his new wife since Hadley had been with him during prior years.

Ernest told Waldo he longed for the bullfights, especially on Sunday around 5:00 PM—it was the first time he had missed the festival since 1923. How he wished he could be there instead of in Wyoming writing his book, and he vowed to see more toros again.

In 1925 he'd gone to the bullfights with Paris friends Harold Loeb, Lady Duff Twysden, and her fiancé Pat Guthrie. When he returned to the apartment above the sawmill where he lived with Hadley and Bumby, he sat down just before his twenty-sixth birthday to write the story of Lady Brett Ashley and the unconsummated love affair with Jake Barnes, finishing the first draft on September 21.

He modeled some of the characters in the book, originally called *Fiesta*, on his friends, and they had felt betrayed. Harold Loeb, Kitty's boyfriend, had been terribly hurt, wondering what he'd ever done to Ernest to deserve this treatment. Kitty never spoke to Ernest again, which

---

* hangover, a condition Ernest frequently suffered.
** Waldo Peirce became known as the American Renoir.

was fine with him because he didn't like her. Duff appeared to take it in stride, but then Ernest mostly stopped seeing her and that crowd altogether. It was during that time he'd met Pauline and a new group of friends: Waldo Peirce, Scott and Zelda Fitzgerald, John Dos Passos, Sara and Gerald Murphy, and Ada and Archie MacLeish.

His new book about the war also had characters based on real people. The nurse, Catherine Barkley, shared characteristics of Agnes von Kurowsky, his first true love and heartbreak. As in *The Sun Also Rises*, he was writing fiction and, as such, was free to borrow details from real life but could make up as much as he wanted. That's something his friends who saw themselves in *The Sun Also Rises* hadn't understood: the characters may have resembled them, and some of the stories he told may have been based on what happened in Pamplona—but it was still fiction. It was important to get the setting right using facts to do so, to make the story believable.

He finished his letter to Waldo, telling his friend that he was lonely without Pauline and that he planned to finish the book before she arrived to join him later that month.

During the day on the ranch when he was working, he was fine, but it was the evenings that got to him. Ernest wanted Pauline to be with him after a day's work, "someone to feel swell with," instead of feeling "just horribly cock-eyed lonesome." He described it as a feeling that rose up "like fog coming up from a river bottom." He didn't do well being alone; the last time he was separated from Pauline for this long he didn't do well at all.

Back in October 1926, Ernest should have been celebrating the success of *The Sun Also Rises*, yet he wasn't feeling celebratory; he felt like his life was falling apart. Pauline was in Piggott, serving out Hadley's hundred-day separation ultimatum, and he was alone in Paris. At first, he and Pauline had written ardent, loved-filled letters to each other, and those had helped him get through the long days. But when Hadley found out about their correspondence, she told them there was to be *no* communication between them for the hundred days; that was the deal. So they had to resort to sneaking messages through Jinny and in telegrams written in code with words like "bears," "Jesuits," and "cubists." "Started" meant Hadley was starting divorce proceedings, and "hurry" from Ernest or "coming" from Pauline meant they were to reunite immediately.

Over time, though, Ernest noticed that the tone of Pauline's letters had changed. He used to be "cockeyed happy" when a letter came, but then she started sounding like the Piggott Chamber of Commerce newsletter, sharing news of domestic events that he didn't care about. He needed her to reassure him that she loved him, and he feared that she was changing her mind. He was so despondent that maybe he had lost Hadley *and* Pauline that he wrote, "Last fall I said perfectly calmly and not bluffingly [a]nd during one of the good times that if this wasn't cleared up by christmas [*sic*] I [w]ould kill myself."

He'd told Pauline during that time, "I love you so Pfife . . . and what I miss worse is not having intimacy with you—nor any feeling of us against the others." He had needed her there with him so he wouldn't have to be alone. What a relief it had been when Hadley called off the hundred-day ultimatum, saying she'd move forward with the divorce and Ernest and Pauline were free to be together.

Soon Pauline would arrive in Wyoming and it would be them against the others again. He just wished she'd hurry.

WEDDING PANTS

PAULINE RECEIVED A CALL from the Piggott operator with a telegram: Ernest had ordered her some "wedding pants" for her upcoming trip to Wyoming. Wedding pants? What could they be? For her wedding in Paris she'd worn an off-white chemise—not pants—with a string of pearls. Her hair was cropped in the popular Paris fashion, the way she still wore it today. And Ernest had looked so handsome in his three-piece tweed suit.

What an intoxicating time it had been, once Ernest's divorce from Hadley was final and they were free to start planning their own wedding. As a Catholic who took her beliefs seriously, living with a devout family in Paris, attending Mass without fail, and avoiding meat on Fridays, Pauline insisted on a wedding sanctioned by the Roman Catholic Church. Her requirement meant that Ernest, who had been raised a Protestant, needed to produce a baptism certificate from the Roman Catholic Church. Ernest explained he had received last rites from a Catholic priest, entering into communion with the Catholic church when he was hospitalized in Milan. He would need to travel to Italy with his friend Guy Hickok, a writer for the *Brooklyn Daily Eagle* based in Paris, to find that priest, hoping he would provide the proof that Ernest needed.

Pauline hadn't wanted him to go; surely there must have been another way to secure the necessary proof. As much as she admired what Ernest was willing to do for her, she had only just reunited with her true love after their separation, when he announced he was leaving for Italy. Was he punishing her for taking too long to return? She knew he had been hurt that she'd taken a month to return to Paris after receiving word that

Hadley had agreed to a divorce, spending Christmas with her extended family in New York City first. He'd told her he understood, but she knew he had hoped she would get on the very next ship from the United States, as they had planned the minute she heard that Hadley had called off the separation. Was his trip to Italy a payback to see how it felt to be left behind?

While Ernest was in Italy, Pauline stayed busy. Her first order of business was to find a place for them to live. She found a gorgeous flat on Rue Ferou, a quiet street near the Luxembourg Gardens. Uncle Gus offered to help finance the lease for the apartment (which she and Ernest continued to lease while they were back in the States, keeping it available for future visits). Jinny had also returned to Paris, and the two of them had shopped for furnishings and decorated it with lovely antiques and rugs.

They also cleaned Ernest's bachelor pad—a.k.a. Gerald Murphy's studio—while Ernest was gone, returning it to pristine shape. Pauline sorted Ernest's clothes for washing and mending, organized his papers and letters—and realized that they would need to hire a maid to help with their new life together.

Sara and Gerald Murphy had been supportive of the relationship between Ernest and Pauline, despite its complications. They liked Hadley well enough, but felt Ernest needed a more sophisticated wife when he took his place in the world as the best writer of his time, and thought Pauline was his perfect match.

Pauline missed Ernest terribly while he was in Italy, writing, "If you will just come back to me you can have your own way all the time. I shall cross you in nothing." He had returned early—ostensibly because he and Guy got into an argument on the trip—and Pauline had kept her promise to this day, continuing to let him have his way and shaping her life around his needs.

Once Ernest was back in Paris, there had been more work to do to appease the Roman Catholic Church: his marriage to Hadley had to be annulled. Since he and Hadley had not been married in the Catholic church, an annulment was granted, though it made Bumby a bastard in the eyes of the church since it meant he had been born out of wedlock.

Pauline was sorry about Bumby, but knew she had sinned by having an affair with Ernest and would need to make amends with God. She had no intention of committing the sin of marrying outside the church.

On May 10, 1927, nearly two years after that fateful tea at Kitty's, Pauline and Ernest were married in a Catholic ceremony in the side chapel of Saint Honoré on the Place Victor Hugo with Jinny and Ernest's banker, Mike Ward, as attendants.

Now back in the United States, Pauline had traded the Paris days of working for *Vogue*, drinking at the Ritz, and dancing to Cole Porter for her new role as Mrs. Hemingway, a job that although exciting, could be very demanding, and required her to do things that she'd never done before, like heading to the wild west of Wyoming.

When the "wedding pants" package arrived in Piggott she learned that the operator had actually said "wading pants," not wedding pants. They were fishing waders for spending time in Wyoming's rivers. She wrote to Ernest, telling him that she could not wait to wear her wedding pants day and night, even if they made her look like "a duffel bag with feet." Her days of couture in Paris were behind her, at least for now.

TAXI SERVICE

When Bill Horne had asked Ernest to join him at Folly Ranch, he didn't know what to expect, but he was delighted by what they found. He thought it was heaven, or a close facsimile. "With a swell cook, Folly the collie, active trout ponds"—not to mention the girls—it had everything a guy could want.

Bill counted Ernest as one of his best friends. After the war, when Ernest was recovering from a broken heart and living with his parents in Oak Park, Bill had offered "to grubstake* him" in Chicago so he could work on being a writer. Bill had been working in advertising, making a fabulous salary of $200 a month, and had saved $900. He was practically rich; the two of them could easily live on that kind of money. At the time, Bill recognized that Ernest had talent, but had no idea how much.

After Ernest married Hadley and moved to Paris, Bill hadn't seen much of his friend for seven years. In a small world, Bill knew some of Ernest's Paris circle. He had attended Princeton with Harold Loeb, who had become friends with Ernest, playing tennis and drinking wine together, and Harold had helped to get Ernest's first book, *In Our Time*, published by his own publisher, Boni & Liveright. When Ernest had gone to the bullfights in Spain, Harold went too, but Bill knew he'd been hurt when Ernest cast him as the heavy character, Robert Cohn, in *The Sun Also Rises*.

---

* Grubstake: to provide supplies or funds to mining prospectors in exchange for a share in their profits.

Bill thought Ernest was a guy who was dominant "because he was smarter, talked better, and looked better than anyone else." Bill watched the cute Folly Ranch girls fawning over Ernest and understood Ernest's need to get away, to be alone to finish his novel.

Maybe they would have more adventures together now that Ernest was back in the United States. Next time, perhaps, they'd explore the Clarks Fork of the Yellowstone that Ernest had pointed out on the map. But it was time for Bill to return to his advertising job in Chicago.

On his last day on the ranch, Eleanor asked a favor. She and some of the Folly Ranch guests were getting ready to depart on a ten-day pack trip deep into the backcountry of the Bighorns, from the Medicine Wheel Ranch, some twenty miles away. She asked Ernest to help shuttle the group to the departure location at Medicine Wheel, and Bill gladly offered to ride with him, giving them time to catch up since he hadn't seen much of Ernie once he'd moved into Sheridan to write.

Eleanor and seventeen Folly campers rode horses seven miles down the mountain to Lower Folly, where Ernest and three additional cars waited for taxi duty. The four-car convoy made a quick stop at Brown Drug in Sheridan for supplies, then headed up "the highest mountain," as Eleanor described it, stopping midway on the steep climb during a brief rainstorm for lunch. The drive to Medicine Wheel Ranch, which they had been told was twenty miles, turned out to be forty miles, because someone had miscalculated the distance. The campers and their drivers got lost before finally bumping across a pasture to arrive at their destination in the late afternoon.

As soon as they reached the ranch, Ernest and Bill had to turn around and head back down the mountain. As Bill said farewell to his new Folly friends, he vowed to stay in touch, particularly with Eleanor's first cousin Bunny Thorne.

Ernest sits with Frances "Bunny" Thorne on his Model A in the Bighorns, 1928.

The Wyoming Room, Sheridan County Public Library System

A VISIT TO OAK PARK

THE NEXT MORNING, after breakfast at Lower Folly, Ernest drove Bill to the depot and they said their goodbyes. Perhaps he would see Horney again this fall—Ernest hadn't been home in years, and he wanted to take Pauline and Patrick to Oak Park to visit his parents and show off his new son, maybe meeting up with Bill then.

Ernest had seen his parents recently, however, if only briefly, during a chance encounter the previous spring in Key West. Before leaving Paris, Ernest had written to his parents to let them know that he and Pauline were heading to Key West for a few months, then traveling to Piggott to visit Pauline's family, and, finally, continuing to Kansas City for the baby's birth. His parents, however, had already left Oak Park on a trip of their own, and didn't receive Ernest's letter. They were traveling to Florida with Clarence's brother, Will, who had convinced Clarence to invest a large portion of the family's savings in Florida real estate. Clarence was alarmed that their investment had lost much of its original value and he wanted to check it out for himself.

One morning, Ernest had been fishing off the P&O pier when he looked down the boardwalk and could not believe his eyes. There, his parents and Uncle Will were walking toward him—turned out they had decided to spend a day sightseeing in Key West. Ernest couldn't believe his good luck to run into them. He called Pauline at the hotel and told her about his surprise, and that they'd be picking her up to spend the day together. It would be Pauline's first time meeting his parents.

The introduction was awkward at first. After all, Clarence had once called Pauline "a love pirate" who had broken up Ernest's family. By day's end, though, feelings had been soothed and his parents softened toward Pauline, who was going to be the mother of their grandchild. Grace Hemingway, in the typical self-absorbed fashion that annoyed Ernest, spent much of the day talking about herself and her newest passion: painting. She was determined to get her work into a Paris show and asked Ernest for his help. In contrast to his mother's exuberance, Ernest thought his father seemed distracted and appeared rather frail, which concerned Ernest.

Ernest had a soft spot for his father, the man who had taught him to love nature and who gently encouraged him to use his talent to write stories that were unlike *The Sun Also Rises*. But Ernest felt his mother was always ready to believe the worst about him and was not loyal. As much as he didn't relish spending time with her, he would like to see his father again soon. He'd need to talk to Pauline to see if they could fit in a visit to Oak Park, since they were planning to travel to Paris in the fall.

MAXIMUM INSURANCE

AFTER DEPOSITING BILL at the Sheridan train depot, Ernest stopped at the post office in Big Horn. The little town, with its false-front general store and post office, had once been a bustling outpost on a popular stagecoach route to Montana's gold mines. These days it was nearly a ghost town, the sort of place one might half expect to see tumbleweeds blowing through, with hardly a soul in sight.

The historic Big Horn Post Office building was built with a false front.
The Wyoming Room, Sheridan County Public Library System

When he picked up his mail he found an insured package from Piggott, Arkansas, waiting for him. His manuscript. He'd left it in Piggott, afraid to travel with it after the terrible loss he had experienced years ago when his manuscripts had been stolen at a train station in Paris. He'd asked Pauline to send it to him after he was settled, and she had insured it for $1,000, the maximum value available. She enclosed a letter, joking, "It cost me $2.38, almost what a baby costs." She wanted him to know that she realized its great worth.

In December 1922 Ernest, then married to Hadley, was working as a stringer for the *Toronto Sun* in Paris when he received an assignment to cover the Lausanne Peace Conference in Switzerland. He and Hadley had fought about it; she didn't want him going off on assignment and leaving her alone in a strange city again. Why did he need to go when they had her trust fund to live on? She didn't understand why he needed to take these jobs. To make up with her, Ernest asked her to meet him at Chamby-sur-Montreux, Switzerland, where they could take a winter vacation after he'd finished.

As she packed, Hadley had an idea. She knew how Ernest loved to work in the morning—how happy it made him—so she decided to surprise him by bringing all his manuscripts, everything he'd written before and during Paris, including carbon copies. Why she had felt the need to bring the carbon copies too was still a mystery to Ernest, but she had. At the Gare de Lyon, she went inside the train station to get a drink of water and when she returned to her train compartment, the suitcase was gone. At first she had thought that she must be in the wrong compartment, but after getting a porter to help her search, reality sunk in. The case had been stolen.

When Hadley's train arrived in Switzerland, Ernest tried to concentrate on her words, to make sense of what was she telling him, but she was crying so hard he couldn't understand her. When he finally realized she was saying they were gone, all gone, he took the next train back to Paris to check for himself and found the manuscript drawer empty.

Gertrude Stein told him, "Start over and concentrate," and that's what he'd done. He had suffered a great loss and it was painful, but in the end he thought some of the stories were even better when he'd rewritten them. Still, as much as he'd tried to forgive Hadley, it had changed his relationship with her. And since that day, he'd become very careful about his manuscripts and keeping them safe.

Back at the ranch house, Ernest read over the manuscript, 575 pages in all, and he was so pleased that he drank nearly a gallon of wine and a half-gallon of beer and forgot to eat supper. The next morning he awoke with gastric remorse, so he wrote letters.

First he wrote to his childhood friend and neighbor Isabelle Simmons Godolphin that Pauline would be coming out in a week, and that he was thankful because he feared he was beginning to get "sheepherder's madness," that fabled affliction caused by lack of female companionship, where the sheep start to look attractive. Ernest knew they would need to follow the doctor's advice and be very careful and scheduled so Pauline didn't get pregnant again for three years. Gone was the spontaneity they had enjoyed before Patrick's conception, but he would just be happy to have Pauline by his side again.

He wrote to Maxwell Perkins, reporting that he'd only fished three times since he arrived because he was "driven by the writing"—on page 575, and it seemed good. He told his editor he would be "awfully happy" when he'd finished the book and could have some family life again, and asked Mr. Perkins to send copies of *Men Without Women* and *The Sun Also Rises* to Howard L. Vickery at the *Sheridan Post Enterprise*. Always concerned about money, he asked about sales of *Men Without Women* before closing.

ANGEL CHILD

PAULINE'S STOMACH WAS FLAT AGAIN. She had worked hard to lose the weight because she'd seen what had happened when Hadley didn't lose her pregnancy weight after Bumby. She was getting her strength back, too, by climbing the stairs. There was nothing she could do about the gigantic scar across her abdomen from the caesarean, but Ernest thought she was brave. She had earned her war wound after eighteen hours of labor.

Now she was doing everything her mother and the doctor ordered to prepare for the trip. "Hurry up and send for your wife, I'll even pay for my own passage," she joked in a letter to Ernest.

To pass the time until she could leave, Pauline entertained herself by writing to Ernest, packing clothes for the trip, and planning Patrick's baptism. Ernest had given his permission for the baptism to take place even though he couldn't be there—he understood Pauline couldn't depart for Wyoming until she'd reserved Patrick's place in heaven.

On August 14, Patrick Miller Hemingway was baptized in the Pfeiffers' home chapel. Pauline wrote to Ernest, "He didn't make a noise until the priest said 'Patrick, do you renounce the Devil with all his works and prophets,' and he gave a little groan and a little whine of protest. Ernest, he is an *angel* child. He never had the colic once, and he hardly ever cries. . . . I think we may like him very much."

Some mothers might have had reservations about leaving their two-month-old baby with family for a whole month, but Pauline didn't. Jinny was doing a fine job of raising Patrick. In fact, it sometimes seemed like Jinny had more maternal instincts than Pauline did. The doctor said Patrick was gaining weight too fast, so Jinny had stopped Patrick's two o'clock formula feedings and started him on orange juice.

Ernest believed nurses and grandparents could raise a baby just as well as he and Pauline could, and Pauline had never been a mother before, so what did she know? First and foremost, Pauline was Ernest's wife, and he'd made it clear that he needed her with him.

FATHERHOOD

BUMBY HAD BEEN BORN when Ernest was only twenty-four years old, and he had felt unprepared to be a father. Now, at age twenty-nine, he had another son to care for. Ernest didn't believe that a child should interfere in the relationship of the couple—the couple should come first. Sometimes, when he and Hadley had gone out alone in Paris, they had left Bumby in the care of their trustworthy cat, F. Puss, a very good babysitter.* Patrick would be in good hands, too, with Pauline's family back in Piggott while Pauline and Ernest enjoyed some time alone together in Wyoming.

He didn't understand people like his friend Waldo Peirce, who was so keen on having children. Ernest had tried to alert Waldo to the perils of fatherhood—Patrick had nearly killed Pauline because he was so large, and then there was the noise to contend with from a bellowing baby. Not to mention, he warned, there was no guarantee children won't grow up to be "shits."

---

* This comes from page 195 in *A Moveable Feast*: "Here were no baby-sitters then and Bumby would stay happy in his tall cage bed with his big, loving cat named F. Puss. There were people who said that it was dangerous to leave a cat with a baby. The most ignorant and prejudiced said the cat would suck a baby's breath and kill him. Others said that a cat would lie on a baby and the cat's weight would smother him. F. Puss lay beside Bumby in the tall cage bed and watched the door with his big yellow eyes, and would let no one come near him while we were out. . . . There was no need for baby-sitters. F. Puss was the baby-sitter."

Ernest planned to be there for the important things, raising his sons as his father had done for him—teaching them to shoot and fish, to love being in the outdoors. But he only half-joked when he said parenting was a part-time job, with nannies, nurses, grandparents, and aunts to help out.

Ernest's relationship with his own father was good enough, but he'd been disappointed that he hadn't been invited to the family's Michigan retreat this summer. When Ernest had written to inquire about visiting before the baby was born, his father had not seemed open to the idea. He advised that Pauline give birth in St. Louis or Kansas City.

As Ernest worked now to finish his manuscript, he thought perhaps this book would be a story his father would enjoy. While his father had tried to be kind in his assessment of *The Sun Also Rises*, his mother was more concerned about what the Oak Park people would think about the book.

When he finished his writing for the day, he looked for entertainment in the afternoon. He'd made friends with Eleanor's cousin Gaylord Donnelley, and the two of them spent time talking, fishing, and visiting Sheridan's bootleggers.

IMPROVISING

GAYLORD DONNELLEY HAD BEEN SPENDING his past three summer breaks from Yale working at Folly Ranch. Although his cousin Eleanor was ten years older, she was his dear friend, always looking out for him. When she bought the ranch, she invited him to visit, promising room and board in exchange for his service as handyman, chore boy, chauffeur, assistant wrangler, assistant guide, stove tender, and whatever other jobs needed to be done.

On his way back to the ranch after doing errands in Sheridan, Gaylord often stopped by Lower Folly, where Ernie was "batching it." Gaylord knew Ernest's typical schedule was to work from 6:00 AM until noon, and that he welcomed male company in the afternoon. Gaylord found Ernest kind, friendly, and extremely likable despite their age difference. When Gaylord shared his aspirations, Ernest had been optimistic about Gaylord's future prospects in academia or business.

On their afternoon jaunts, the two men patronized several local brewers in Sheridan. One was Sheridan's street cleaner, who patrolled the street with a can on wheels. A request would be made, a rendezvous point established, and the street cleaner would retrieve moonshine in brown bags from inside the manure can. Gaylord thought the pints were "not much worse for the association."

Another secret spot in town was a wonderful cool bar in the basement of Brown's Drugstore, reached through a trapdoor at the rear of the building. Gaylord found the establishment's gin fizz to be especially delicious on a day when the thermometer outside was over a hundred degrees.

On a fishing trip with Ernest to a fly camp at Cross Creek in the Bighorns, located just below the snowcapped Cloud Peak, Gaylord learned a lot about fly-fishing—and also about improvising. Ernest taught him that when in need of a flask, a baby's bottle could be filled with whiskey, and it didn't break when it was dropped on a rock in the river.

Ernie was always a lot of fun to be around, and one Sunday afternoon a group from Folly got together: Gaylord, his friend Bill Poole, a lovely friend of Eleanor's named Josie Wall Merck (who was divorced), and Ernest. Over a jug of beer, Ernest entertained the group as the three men vied for Josie's attention. Gaylord had known Josie for several years and had even visited her in New York, thinking he might have the inside track to her affections. But he could see that even Josie was not immune to Ernest's charms. Gaylord couldn't be mad; he liked Ernest and considered him a new friend. Gaylord hoped that one day when Ernest was in the East, he might even visit him at Yale.

WAITING FOR PAULINE

On August 18, as Ernest pulled out of the driveway at Lower Folly, his characters Frederic and Catherine were in a hospital delivery room with Catherine's labor pains. Ernest was on page 600, about two days from the end, and although he had tried to finish it before Pauline arrived, he was stuck, trying to get the words right.

On the veranda of the Sheridan Inn, waiting for Pauline's train, which was almost two hours late, he wrote letters as the anticipation was killing him. It had been three weeks since he'd seen his wife, too many nights sleeping alone. He looked forward to showing her the Wyoming he'd discovered—the Bighorn Mountains and locals like the French bootleggers. Pauline would enjoy sitting on the couple's porch, drinking wine and speaking French with them.

When Pauline finally stepped off the train—her dark hair cropped, figure in shape, no outward signs of the time she'd been through—Ernest was thrilled. He took her to a party at the Hortons' HF Bar dude ranch with a number of Folly friends, who later reported that "Mrs. Ernie," as the Folly crowd called her, was "a smooth number who danced the Charleston."

The next day they drove up Red Grade Road ten miles past Folly Ranch, where Ernest turned the roadster down a gravel road and stopped outside a lodge built in the shape of a spear, with a point and shaft. Located at 8,300 feet, Spear-O-Wigwam was another dude ranch, this one owned by Senator Willis Spear; he'd hired a New York architect to design the complicated structure shaped like the Spear cattle brand. The

53

An aerial view of Spear-O-Wigwam, the lodge was built in the shape of an arrow. *The Wyoming Room, Sheridan County Public Library System*

Welcome to the Spear-O-Wigwam. *Courtesy Travis Cebula*

The massive fireplace at the Spear-O-Wigwam anchors the room. *Courtesy Travis Cebula*

lodge housed the kitchen, dining hall, and a communal area large enough to accommodate two hundred people, with a massive stone fireplace in the center. On the walls, mounted heads, hides, antlers, Indian relics, and muzzle-loading guns were hung for décor.

Ernest and Pauline were escorted to the Rosebud Cabin—a rustic pole-log cabin with two bedrooms and a bathroom, their home for the next week. Although it didn't have a fireplace, it had a cozy stove and a view of a bubbling stream from the bedroom; they could open the windows and hear the water rushing past. The furniture was made from logs, and Ernest could write at a desk tucked beneath the window. The cabin had a front deck with chairs positioned to take in the view of the distant peaks.

On their arrival, Ernest took a day off from writing to explore the ranch with Pauline. But the next day he needed to get back to work on the book's ending, so he sent Pauline fishing with a guide and sat down at the desk in the Rosebud Cabin to write.

The rustic Rosebud Cabin at Spear-O-Wigwam circa 1930. Its name was later changed to the Hemingway Cabin. *The Wyoming Room, Sheridan County Public Library System*

Ernest wrote beneath the cabin window, writing some thirty-nine endings for *A Farewell to Arms*. *Courtesy Travis Cebula*

FRESH MOUNTAIN AIR

PAULINE DIDN'T MIND being on her own, acquainting herself with the land. The fresh air was therapeutic, and the freedom she felt was intoxicating after being confined for so long. In Wyoming, she felt strong again, and she was determined to keep up with Ernest as they hunted and fished their way across the state.

Pauline was delighted to receive a letter from Jinny shortly after her arrival, reporting on Patrick's progress. Jinny was trying to get Patrick "raised" by the time they returned from Wyoming. Patrick ruled the household, everyone doted on his needs. He let them know his displeasure if he wasn't put out on the swing at 4:00 PM, crying until he got his way.

Jinny described his many attributes, saying, he had "handsome eyes, a mouth like Bumby's, and beautiful skin that browned in the sun." She said she'd found a Dutch product called KLEEN that kept his knees clean.

Jinny and her friend Ayleene Spence liked to push Patrick in his carriage to Piggott Square and show him off to merchants and friends. They stopped at the soda fountains in Reve's Drug Store and Porters's Drug Store, so the ladies who gathered there in the afternoon for cherry Cokes could admire baby Patrick.

Pauline knew Patrick was surrounded by love and being perfectly cared for, making it easier for her to be away. Ernest expected this of her; he'd been the same with Hadley too, demanding that they leave Bumby with his nurse, sometimes for months. This was only the first time she would need to choose between her husband and her child. She knew there would be more times to come. And she would choose Ernest.

On the way to Wyoming, Pauline had stopped in St. Louis to visit her dentist. She overheard women gossiping about the writer Ernest Hemingway—that he had married his second wife, also from St. Louis like his first. The women speculated that the character Lady Brett Ashley in his scandalous novel *The Sun Also Rises* must have been based on his new wife. Pauline was amused, but she didn't correct them to say that the character was actually based on Lady Duff Twysden.

Just as Ernest's crush on Duff had been the inspiration behind *The Sun Also Rises*, his previous love for Agnes von Kurowsky had inspired his new book, but this didn't bother Pauline. She understood that writers and artists needed inspiration, and she didn't care where it came from as along as Ernest was hers.

While at Spear-O-Wigwam, Pauline met the Spears' daughter Elsa, who had just returned from a pack trip. The people at the ranch couldn't have been nicer to Pauline. In the mornings she rode with them into the pristine wilderness around the ranch, along trails to crystal-clear lakes and streams. After her adventures, Pauline always came back in time to bring Ernest lunch or to do anything he asked. She looked forward to the time when he would finish the book so she would have him to herself.

THE END

So close. As Ernest sat in the little log cabin and tried on different endings, weighing different options, he was ready to finish the bloody book. He wrote in a frenzy for three days, beginning the day with breakfast at the lodge—steak, eggs, red onion, and wine—not speaking to other guests, intent on eating and getting to work. Then he headed back to the cabin to write until Pauline brought him lunch.

On August 23, five days after picking Pauline up from the depot, after multiple attempts, he finally knew what the ending would be. It was inspired by Patrick's birth as Ernest had sat helplessly by, fearing that both Patrick and Pauline would die. Ernest finished the first draft.

The feeling was exhilarating. Ernest would put the book aside and let it cool off for a while before he started the revision, something that was pretty important and would take between six weeks and two months—at least that's how long it had taken him to edit *The Sun Also Rises*. He was now free to fish and drink and have fun with Pauline. She wore her "wedding pants," and they caught thirty trout apiece every day.

1928

A rustic but comfortable writing place at Spear-O-Wigwam. *The Wyoming Room, Sheridan County Public Library System*

SEEING D'AMERICA

On August 24, the *Sheridan Journal* reported: "Ernest Hemingway, writer of prominence and author of the new novel 'Men Without Women' that is meeting with such demand in the east, is a guest at the Wigwam lodge. Mr. Hemingway is accompanied by Mrs. Hemingway and for the past three years they have made their home in Paris."

Ernest and Pauline were leaving Spear-O-Wigwam, however, now that his book was finished, to see more of the Cowboy State. They drove over the top of the Bighorns, past the turnoff to Medicine Wheel Ranch, where Ernest and Bill had deposited the Folly packers, through pastures of late-blooming wildflowers. They swerved around hairpin curves in Shell Canyon, a deep chasm carved out of sedimentary stone and granite, and heard the roar of the waterfall before they came upon it as it plunged one hundred twenty feet to the canyon floor. The magnificent walls in the canyon eventually opened to the small town of Shell, population fifty, their first stop.

Owen Wister, author of *The Virginian*, considered by many to be the first true Western novel, was staying near Shell. He was a guest at Trapper Creek Lodge, built in 1927 by the Wyeth family of Wyeth Pharmaceuticals on a dude ranch they'd purchased the previous year. Maxwell Perkins had recommended that Ernest visit Wister, saying that Wister would be delighted to meet Ernest, and indeed Ernest found him a "sweet old guy." They made plans to connect when they were both in Paris, possibly even later that fall when the Hemingways were anticipating being there.

From Shell, Ernest and Pauline drove through a ranching valley near Greybull in the white-hot light of August, passing through wild mustang country near Cody. The area, called the Bighorn Basin, had been discovered by explorer John Colter in 1807. The ancient land was unlike any place else on earth, mostly uninhabited and otherworldly, with massive red rock formations where fossils and dinosaur bones had been found.

Some of the houses they passed were no more than shacks. Wyoming had been going through an economic slump, with much of the state's revenue coming from tourism driven by the popularity of car travel. Ernest liked to tell his friends he was "Seeing D'America," a spoof on the national advertising campaign "See America First," encouraging Americans to take car trips and see the country in all its glory. The newfound popularity of dude ranches, along with the attraction of Yellowstone National Park, helped draw guests to the state to support the economy. Even so, many residents, like the Sheridan bootleggers and other working-class people, struggled to make a living.

Ernest and Pauline fished in the Sunlight River and the Clarks Fork, that lonely little river near the Montana state line, between the Absaroka and Beartooth Mountains, that Ernest and Bill had spotted on the map at Folly Ranch. Jackson Hole, their next stop, was over two hundred miles away through Yellowstone National Park. They were headed to the Bar BC Ranch, owned by another Scribner's author, Maxwell Struthers Burt, who wrote *Diary of a Dude Wrangler* and *The Delectable Mountains*. The ranch was popular with an East Coast literary crowd, including the prominent publisher Alfred Knopf. As a Princeton alumnus, Struthers also hosted many affluent Eastern city dwellers.

An advocate for the unspoiled American West, Struthers had owned and operated the Bar BC Ranch since 1912. He was a "furious foe of Prohibition" and had written about it in an essay, "The Dry West," that appeared in the February 1928 issue of *Scribner's Magazine*.

As Ernest and Pauline neared Jackson Hole, they entered a valley surrounded by the Gros Ventre and Teton Ranges—giving the area its name "hole." The Snake River curved through the valley floor with ancient cottonwoods lining its banks. Ernest and Pauline drove east through sagebrush flats, toward the river, the jagged Tetons towering above them. They passed a charming chapel built miles from civilization on the valley floor, the Chapel of the Transfiguration, with a window that framed the view of the stunning peaks.

When they reached a bench of land, they dropped down to a terrace where the Bar BC stretched along the Snake River. Nestled against the hill, invisible from above, the compound included cabins, a lodge, a dining hall, a laundry/utility building, corrals, man-made pools, and an assortment of barns, sheds, and log structures with red or green roofs.

Struthers gave the Hemingways a cabin with a porch that faced the magnificent Snake River, where Pauline and Ernest fished, catching "three big ones"—two-, two-and-a-half-, and three-pound cutthroat trout. But they arrived too early in the season; the water was running high and they couldn't wade. Ernest heard fishing was grand at the end of September when they shut off the dam.

Ernest was "cockeyed" about shooting, never traveling without three guns. He'd brought his .22-caliber Colt automatic pistol, a .410-gauge shotgun, and a .12-gauge Winchester pump to Wyoming. On the drive back to Sheridan, Ernest entertained himself by shooting prairie dogs from the car.

The cabin where Ernest and Pauline stayed at the Bar BC as it looks today, restored by Grand Teton National Park. *Courtesy Katherine Wonson, 2012*

MONEY IN THE BANK

IT WAS EARLY SEPTEMBER when Ernest and Pauline returned to Sheridan, checking into the Sheridan Inn to wait for prairie chicken season to open on September 15. Senator Spear had invited them to join his camp in the Wolf Mountains on the Crow Indian Reservation for the shoot. Ernest found a letter from Maxwell Perkins waiting for him at the post office with a check for $3,718.66—royalties from *Men Without Women*. He was happy to have the money; his earnings were down to ninety dollars per month, and life was expensive.

He wrote to Mr. Perkins to thank him for the letter and the check, and to inform him that the first draft of the book was finished. He shared his Wyoming adventures, describing how much the country reminded him of Spain. The only thing he didn't like, he told his editor, were dude ranches: dreadful places—he could write a story about them. Finally, he noted that he and Pauline would be returning to Piggott the following week, then heading to Key West for the winter to revise the new novel.

Without a book to work on, Ernest caught up on his correspondence. He wrote on Sheridan Inn stationery to Waldo Peirce, Guy Hickok, and Archibald MacLeish with updates about Patrick (he weighed sixteen pounds), wonderful fishing (they caught thirty trout apiece each day for nearly a week), and Pauline (she was feeling strong again) and signed his letters respectively, "Yours in haste HEM," "Yours always Ernest," and "Pappy."

He wrote to his sister Madelaine ("Sunny"), telling her he and Pauline had decided to postpone their trip to Paris until the spring; instead, they would be staying in Key West so Ernest could finalize his book there. They didn't have a home—living in hotels, with relatives, on ranches— and felt they needed to stay in one place this winter. Key West was a fine place to work, and Sunny was invited to come down and stay once they found a house to rent. She could come with them to Paris when they decided to go. He signed off, "Your always Bro Ernie."

He sent his friend Sylvia Beach in Paris, founder of Shakespeare and Company bookstore, a postcard with a drawing of a sheepherder on the front, telling her that he and Pauline had a son named Patrick and that the new book was done.

Before leaving for the prairie chicken hunt in Montana, Ernest and Pauline visited their Sheridan bootlegger friends and told them they were heading to the Crow Reservation. The French couple asked them to be sure to come back after hunting, when the wine would be ready.

A LADY IN THE CAR

PAULINE AND ERNEST awoke early on September 14 and dressed, both wearing white button-down shirts and belted dungarees with the legs cuffed, and little black berets, then drove an hour to the Wolf Mountains to meet Willis Spear and his crew. They piled in Spear's car to ride with

Ernest and Pauline at hunting camp on the Crow Indian Reservation, 1928.
The Wyoming Room, Sheridan County Public Library System

Pauline with her pistol in a holster. She was determined to hunt and fish and keep up with Ernest, 1928. *Ernest Hemingway Collection, John F. Kennedy Presidential Library and Museum, Boston*

him, and he stopped to speak to a sheepherder. Sheepherders often lived by themselves on the range without seeing another soul for months, so they weren't accustomed to company. This sheepherder was using some colorful language.

"Now, now, there's a lady in the car," Spear reprimanded.

The herder peered into the car, looking into the back seat, and defended himself, saying, "I don't see no lady!"

With her cropped hair and boyish figure, wearing dungarees and a beret, Pauline probably did look like a boy, and she laughed off the sheepherder's comment.

At camp, Pauline was delighted to see her friend Elsa Spear and Elsa's mother, who had traveled to the camp to enjoy a prairie chicken dinner

Ernest sitting on the wheel well as Senator Willis Spear and his party prepare to hunt prairie chickens, 1928. *The Wyoming Room, Sheridan County Public Library System*

that night. While at Spear-O-Wigwam, Elsa had not appreciated Ernest's cussing or what she considered his lack of manners when he pointed at the food he wanted and sometimes grabbed things from Pauline's hands. But she, like most everyone, was converted to Ernest's charms—she came to understand that was just Ernest; it was hard to get mad at him. It was lucky the hunting party had shot nine prairie chickens that day, enough to feed the large group.

A FAREWELL TO WYOMING

DESPITE THEIR LUCK on the first day of hunting, on the second day they hadn't seen a single prairie chicken. Ernest and Pauline returned to Sheridan hot and tired—they'd been up since 5:00 AM—and they were thirsty when they finally reached town that afternoon. Ernest turned down the dusty road and stopped at the bootleggers' house. The wife gave them her last two bottles of beer and told them to come back that night—her husband would have the wine.

With their time in Wyoming over, they planned to start the drive back to Piggott the next morning. But there was still much to do: Ernest needed to send his father a telegram and get the car looked over by a mechanic. After dropping the car at the garage, he walked back to the hotel in the heat. When the time came for dinner, he was too tired to see the bootleggers and speak in a foreign language, but there was no way to reach the couple and tell them they wouldn't be coming.

The next morning, Ernest and Pauline both felt guilty about not showing up for dinner, so they decided to stop to say goodbye on the way out of town. Ernest could tell the French couple was disappointed. The husband had been eager to show off the wine he had made. When Ernest and Pauline hadn't shown up for dinner, he'd drunk three bottles himself.

After saying goodbye, Pauline and Ernest drove through the hills outside Sheridan, leaving the Bighorns behind. Ernest's life spread out before him like the road ahead. His new novel seemed good; maybe the critics would even like it. He was itching to revise the book now, but wanted to make sure he waited long enough. Even though he'd finished writing *The Sun Also Rises* in September, he'd waited until December to start the revisions, and he felt that schedule should be repeated.

While he waited, he would use the time to visit his family in Oak Park, Illinois, and he could go to the East Coast to see Scott and Zelda, and Archie and Ada MacLeish—who were back in the States now too—and maybe take in a football game or two. He could even stop by to visit Gaylord Donnelley at Yale.

When he saw his father, he'd tell him about Wyoming and the fish Ernest and Pauline had caught—despite the fact that his father didn't seem as interested in hunting and fishing as he once was. Would his father like his new book? Ernest hated that he had disappointed him with *The Sun Also Rises* and hoped maybe this time he'd like what Ernest wrote.

Just as in his own childhood, when his family escaped Oak Park's heat by spending time at Windemere Cottage on Walloon Lake, Wyoming could be the place where Ernest brought his own family for a retreat, teaching his sons to shoot and fish as his father had done for him.

In the golden September light, as the shadows became longer and the days shorter, Pauline and Ernest drank whiskey and ate apples in a fine cold wind as they drove. Ernest's lips were chapped from the sun and alkali—even worse than in Key West. He had never felt stronger, he was in fine shape, and he hadn't been sick or had an accident since being back in America. When he had told this to Maxwell Perkins, he would need to say "knocking on wood."

He was superstitious and he believed in luck; it was why he carried a worn rabbit's foot in his pocket. Once, long ago in Paris, when he had been married to Hadley, living in the apartment above the dance hall, there had been a moment when he had felt lucky. He should have knocked on wood then. He should always remember to knock on wood.*

----

* When Hemingway penned his fictional memoir, *A Moveable Feast*, at the end of his life, he looked back on his early years in Paris, writing on page 34: "'My,' she said. 'We're lucky that you found the place.' 'We're always lucky,' I said and like a fool I did not knock on wood. There was wood everywhere in that apartment to knock on too."

Part II

1930

What Ernest Loved About Pauline

Keen editorial eye
Her family became his family: Jinny, Mother Pfeiffer
Uncle Gus's support
Strong again
"Someone to feel swell with" after a day's work
The "feeling of us against the others"
Willing to join him on adventures
Believed in the "promotion of masculine society"
Never worried like other wives
Vowed to always let him have his way
She could give him "little Pilar"
~~Her throat never got sore like his~~
~~Spontaneous lovemaking~~

THE L BAR T

In May 1930, the heat arrived in Key West, then hurricane weather, making it impossible to think. Ernest wrote to Waldo, "Have been drinking too since the damned heat came—Had to drink on acct. the heat—Then when the rain set in found a damn good excuse [to] drink on acct. of the rain."

It was time to move to a cooler climate, and Wyoming was a good place to work. He'd written seventy-four pages of a new nonfiction book about bullfighting, but he'd suffered a few delays. First, he'd sliced his index finger clean to the bone on Charlie Thompson's punching bag, requiring six stitches. He couldn't type or hold a pen.

Then he was laid low by the grippe while visiting Pauline's family in Arkansas. He had to stay in bed and dose with quinine, postponing any work on the book and the trip West with Pauline and Bumby, now age six, who was visiting for the summer from Paris. Ernest had met Bumby's ship in New York and started feeling ill on the drive to Arkansas.

While in Piggott, they had celebrated Patrick's second birthday with the Pfeiffers on June 28, in heat just as stifling as in the Keys. Ernest hadn't slept well in forty consecutive hot nights and he would welcome the refreshing mountain air. Ernest, Pauline, and Bumby set out on July 2 for Wyoming. Patrick was too young to come along, so he stayed behind with the Pfeiffers and his French nurse, Henriette, hired last year while they were in Paris.

Their new Model A Ford coupe, with its rumble seat and running boards, was a comfortable touring car, the second from Uncle Gus after Ernest's sister Sunny wrecked the first one while staying with them in

Key West. Ernest had driven this new car to the bullfights in Paris last year with Jinny and Guy Hickok and then shipped it to the States when they returned. Uncle Gus had even offered to buy them a third car—a newer model for the trip West—and although Ernest enjoyed a fine new car, he had demurred. He told Gus this car was still performing fine; why not use the money on more important things? Uncle Gus told Ernest that he understood the wisdom of taking his current car west as long as it was still driving well.

Uncle Gus and his wife Louise didn't have children of their own, so they gave their attention—and money—to their nieces and nephews, wanting to share their wealth, made in pharmaceuticals, with the entire family. Gus and Ernest had struck up a friendship, and Ernest had dedicated *A Farewell to Arms* to him in appreciation of his many kindnesses and support.

The Hemingways stopped in Kansas City at Ernest's relatives, the Lowrys, who had hosted them during Patrick's birth. Then they drove through Nebraska, where it was 108 degrees in the shade as the Midwest and southern Great Plains continued to suffer through a heat wave and drought, contributing to dust storms that further devastated the parched land.*

In addition to the land being dried up, the country's economy had dried up. The Great Depression had begun: banks had been closed, stockbrokers were jumping out windows to their death, families had lost their jobs and their savings and were living in the streets. Ernest stopped along the road to give some of these weary travelers a ride, and they shared their sad tales of loss.

When they reached Sheridan, Ernest determined that the area was too settled—he wanted a place where no one would know him. Since the publication of *A Farewell to Arms* the past fall, people wrote fan letters and were starting to recognize him in public, so he wanted to find a remote location deep in the mountains. Horney had given him a tip about an isolated ranch where he'd heard the "fishing is simply godwonderful." It was near the border between Wyoming and Montana, located on the

---

* The Dust Bowl started in 1930 from poor agricultural practices, sweeping across Western prairies through 1936.

Clarks Fork River, which Ernest and Pauline had fished on their previous trip. It might be the perfect place.

Located in the northwest corner of Wyoming near Yellowstone National Park, the ranch Horney had told them about was a day's drive from Sheridan. Ernest steered the coupe around the boulders and ruts on Red Grade Road as they made their way from Sheridan over the Bighorns while Bumby peered out the window at the precipice, not making a sound. They drove through Shell Canyon and the prehistoric-looking Bighorn Basin, finally reaching Yellowstone National Park's east entrance, only to sit for hours while crews worked to repair the road. When they were finally allowed to enter the park, they headed north, exiting in Montana near the western mining town of Cooke City, and from there took a dirt road ribbed like corduroy back down into Wyoming to land that bordered the park's east side.

The Nordquist Ranch cabins still stand today. *Darla Worden*

Nordquist Ranch was surrounded by rugged land. *Darla Worden*

The view south from Nordquist Ranch. *Darla Worden*

In 1872, when Yellowstone National Park's boundaries had been drawn, it had been impossible to contain all the geological wonders inside; nature colored outside the lines. Rugged volcanic mountains, deep canyon chasms, soaring peaks, and roaring rivers spilled out onto neighboring lands to the east. This was serious country, not for novice outdoorsmen; the secluded and rough land included miles of inaccessible terrain. The area* was famous for wildlife—elk, bighorn sheep, deer, moose, black bears, and grizzlies, the largest predators in the United States—wildlife that Ernest intended to hunt before leaving in October. And it had a reputation for world-class trout fishing. Ernest had said on their 1928 visit that it had been the best he'd experienced.

On July 14 the coupe turned down a dirt road with grass growing between the tracks, through a stand of quaking aspens, then crossed a rickety log bridge that led to a wide open meadow. L Bar T Ranch wrangler Ivan Wallace later told the story that he couldn't believe his eyes—his job was to bring dudes to the ranch by wagon or horseback because the roads were boulder-strewn and impossible. About four miles from the ranch, Ivan would need to tie a log to the back of the wagon so the weight would keep them from tumbling down a steep hill with a deep swamp at the bottom. Yet here was the first car to ford the Clarks Fork River, with a driver looking relaxed as he sped with his wife and young son toward the ranch entrance.

Ernest introduced himself but didn't mention the rocks or the swamp. "I'm a writer looking for a place to work," he said. "My name is Ernest Hemingway."

The wrangler had never heard of him, and that was the way Ernest liked it. Ivan took them to meet Olive Nordquist, who owned the L Bar T with her husband, Lawrence. (The ranch was named by using the first and last letters of his name.) She showed them to a new double cabin she felt would be just right for the family.

---

* In 1964 the area was designated as the North Absaroka Wilderness Area.

JACK'S ROOM

As THEY DROVE across a wide clover meadow near a little grouping of log cabins, Bumby—or "Jack" as he preferred to be called now by everyone except "Papa"—was happy to reach the ranch after being cooped up inside the coupe.

He had started his voyage nearly a month earlier in France with Aunt Jinny after his summer break from school began. Aunt Jinny had been visiting in Paris and had offered to bring him back on the *Lafayette* to New York City, where Papa met the ship. From there they drove to Pauline's family home in Piggott to pick up Pauline, but Papa got sick and they had to stay in town for a while, which was fine with Jack.

Jack couldn't recall a time when Pauline had not been in his life; he felt sorry for other children who only had one mother when he had two marvelous mothers. He gave her the nickname "Paulinoes" when he was small; he would ask his dad a question and Papa would reply, "Ask Pauline, Pauline knows," so Jack thought her name was Paulinoes, and the nickname stuck.

On the way to Wyoming, when they stayed with Pauline's family in Arkansas, the Pfeiffers treated him like one of their own. Jack enjoyed exploring Piggott and experiencing the privileges associated with being the bank president's step-grandson. At the local drugstore he was allowed to charge sodas, and he sampled sweets that weren't available in Paris.

After his dad recovered, they drove from Arkansas through wide open plains, on scary mountain roads near Sheridan, and through Yellowstone National Park. Jack had never seen land like this before except in movies*—cliffs, canyons, buttes, waterfalls. At the L Bar T Ranch, he looked up at two giant peaks towering above the valley floor, like fingers pointing at the sky.

One of the first real cowboys Jack had ever met, Ivan, showed them to a brown log cabin where Jack would have his very own room. Jack went to the corral, the place horses were saddled for rides and brushed after a day on the trails. Ivan sized up Jack and matched him with "Pinky," a white horse with liver-colored speckles. Jack knew he and Pinky would become the best of friends.

---

* Aunt Jinny took Jack to see movies at the cinema in Paris.

PAULINE'S RESPITE

PAULINE BREATHED IN THE SAGE-SCENTED air and felt herself relax. Situated in a valley with a river running through the meadow and a majestic mountain range in view, the ranch was lovely. She'd finally have some time alone with her husband. She had hardly seen him in Key West except for when he came home to get clean clothes. Although she never objected to Ernest's time with his friends, since renting a house in Key West the previous January they'd had an endless stream of visitors, including Maxwell Perkins, Archie MacLeish, Mike Strater, John Hermann, and Burge Saunders. Ernest enjoyed showing them his haunts and taking them deep-sea fishing, but Pauline was prone to seasickness, so sometimes opted out, preferring to stay home and meet the group on the dock at cocktail hour.

At the ranch, no friends would be dropping by, and she'd get a break from caring for a busy toddler. Pauline's family relished the opportunity to host Patrick and Henriette while Pauline and Ernest enjoyed some time alone together in Wyoming, or "Wyo-tana," as Patrick called it. He was a precocious two-year-old who spoke French because he had lived in Paris from the time he was nine months to eighteen months old. When they returned to Key West, he could say only a few English words and phrases, like "hobo" and "I don't know." Pauline's family promised to help him learn more English while his parents were away.

Pauline didn't mind that Jack was with them at the ranch; he'd have his own activities with other children and could run freely while Pauline and Ernest explored the area on their own. When Jack was with them, Pauline kept Hadley up to date on his activities, having

83

Pauline in front of one of the Nordquist cabins. *Ernest Hemingway Collection, John F. Kennedy Presidential Library and Museum, Boston*

managed to partially mend their fractured relationship through her devotion to Jack.

Pauline felt Jack was old enough to have a few responsibilities, so she assigned him two important chores. In the morning, it would be his job to start a fire in the little Franklin stove so the cabin would be warm when she and Ernest got up. He was also given the job of foraging for wild strawberries that grew in the area, filling two tumblers for Pauline's "ranch cocktails" that she made by adding gin. It was still Prohibition, so she and Ernest traveled with their own supply of booze, plus the ranch had connections to local bootleggers if they ran low.

In Paris last year, Pauline had become extremely ill, taking months to recover. She knew she needed to be strong. Ernest admired women who were strong, and she was determined to hunt and fish and ride hard all summer, to show him just how strong she could be. While Ernest worked on his bullfighting book, she donned dungarees and boots and headed to the corral to get outfitted with a horse of her own for a trail ride with the guides under blue Wyoming skies.

THE WORLD CHANGED

ERNEST STOOD ON THE FRONT PORCH of the cabin, squinting up at the mountain peaks as he wiped off his glasses on his shirt. His desk was positioned in a corner of the porch to take in the magnificent views of Index (11,699 feet) and Pilot (11,708 feet) Peaks, the highest in the Absaroka Range. He listened as the Clarks Fork of the Yellowstone River rushed by, literally flowing through his front yard. Ernest had once told F. Scott Fitzgerald that heaven would be his own trout stream that no one else could fish in; at the remote L Bar T Ranch, maybe he had found heaven.

The world had changed since Ernest's previous visit to Wyoming. On December 6, 1928, his father, Clarence Hemingway, had closed the door to his office, put a Civil War pistol to his head, and shot himself, shattering Ernest's family. Ernest hadn't learned it was suicide until he arrived in Oak Park for the funeral. He knew his father had appeared weak when he'd last seen him, but hadn't known that he'd been suffering from angina and diabetes. Clarence had been worrying himself sick about the precarious financial situation he'd created from investing in Florida swampland, a situation he had not shared with his family. He had asked his wealthy brother Will for help, but Will had turned him down. So, out of despair, Clarence had pulled the trigger.

Ernest had been with Bumby on December 6, 1928, when he received word that his father was dead. They were traveling from New York City to Key West, where Bumby would spend the winter with them, away from the damp Paris air. When Ernest received the telegram, he had to act swiftly, making arrangements for Bumby, then only five years old, to continue on the train to Key West by himself in the care of a porter while Ernest traveled to Oak Park for the funeral.

Pauline picked up Bumby from the train station and went into action, sending Ernest and Hadley telegrams that he had arrived. Next, she did her best to comfort Ernest's sister Sunny, who had come to live with them that fall to help with Patrick. Poor Sunny wouldn't be able to make it to Oak Park in time for the funeral, and she took her father's death so hard that Pauline had to call a doctor to give her a sedative.

Ernest had received heartfelt condolences from the Pfeiffer family and a letter from Hadley, who had wanted him to know she was thinking of him. Her own father, James Richardson, had killed himself twenty-five years earlier, so she understood what Ernest was going through. "Taty, I felt so sorry for you, the mixture of emotions! I remember how affectionately you talked of him to me in New York."*

Hadley was his dear friend, despite all they had been through. Ernest knew he had disappointed his parents with the divorce and by leaving Hadley and Bumby, and he'd continued to embarrass them with the rough language used in some of his stories. He wished his father could have seen the wonderful reviews of A Farewell to Arms—maybe he would have been proud of him. But Ernest would never know.

At least he had seen his father one last time before his death. Ernest had made the trip to Oak Park in the fall of 1928 alone, as it had seemed overwhelming to bring a baby to visit, and Pauline needed to spend time with Patrick after being away from him for a month during their Wyoming vacation. It had been a good visit despite the visible change in his father's health, but when Ernest departed, he hadn't realized how bad his father must have been feeling.

As the oldest son, Ernest became the man of the family, left to deal with the finances, the mortgage, and college funds for his siblings. His mother had been clueless about the state of the family's finances and was shocked to find out the dreadful state they were in. Ernest had started sending one hundred dollars a month to help out, which she didn't feel was enough. After the success of A Farewell to Arms, he'd been able to

---

* "Taty" was one of Hadley's pet names for him.

set up a $50,000 trust for her with the help of Pauline and generous Uncle Gus.

––––––––––––

Ernest was feeling pressure with the loss of his father and the need to contribute to his mother's finances, not to mention concern over his own finances. Ernest and Pauline had been back in Paris when *A Farewell to Arms* was published on September 27, 1929, to glowing reviews. James Aswell, critic for the *Richmond Times-Dispatch*, wrote, "I have finished *A Farewell to Arms*, and am still a little breathless as people often are after a major event in their lives."

His friend John Dos Passos had written a review for the *New Masses:*

> Hemingway's *A Farewell to Arms* is the best written book that has seen the light in America for many a long day. I don't mean the tasty college composition course sort of thing that our critics seem to consider good writing. I mean writing that is terse and economical, in which each sentence and each phrase bears it maximum load of meaning, sense impressions, emotions. The book is a firstrate [*sic*] piece of craftsmanship by a man who knows his job. It gives you the sort of pleasure line by line that you get from handling a piece of wellfinished [*sic*] carpenter's work.

The book was even being dramatized in a play opening in New York. Ernest wasn't part of that venture, though, because of his focus on writing his bullfighting book. His agent did get him a small fee plus a cut of the profits if it succeeded. To make money on *A Farewell to Arms*, Ernest would have to sell sixty thousand copies before he earned out his advance and started receiving royalties—money he needed to support Hadley and Bumby, Pauline and Patrick, and his mother and siblings.

On October 29, 1929, financial matters had become even worse with Black Tuesday, the ensuing stock market crash, and the beginning of the

Great Depression. People couldn't afford to feed their families, so how could they buy books?

The Piggott State Bank, where Paul Pfeiffer served as president, permanently closed its doors after a run on the bank in February 1930. However, within days of the bank's closing, a group of businessmen created a new bank called Arkansas State Bank, with Pauline's parents, Paul and Mary, acting jointly as president to get it running before turning it over to a younger group of managers. Paul's real estate holdings had suffered too; profits were dwindling from his large tracts of land dependent upon tenant farmers, so he sold much of his land to the federal government. Still, despite some setbacks, the Pfeiffers' finances were in much better shape than those of many Americans.

As these events unfolded, publisher Nelson Doubleday made it even harder to make a living as a writer by announcing he would cut the price of Doubleday books from two dollars to one dollar, and other publishers followed to stay competitive. Ernest thought the publishing business was just about "belly up," and he joked that maybe he'd have to change careers and open a retail and wholesale fish business.

Ernest had sold only one story in 1930: "Wine of Wyoming," to *Scribner's Magazine*, about the French bootleggers he'd met in Sheridan. When he was writing a book, he couldn't stop to write articles and stories for magazines—he needed to focus on the book. Pauline had typed up the story—a whopping six thousand words. Ernest knew it was long and that Max (he no longer called him Mr. Perkins) would object to the French dialogue he included.

Ernest convinced Max by saying everyone that read *Scribner's* knew a little French and that the French was necessary to the story. Ernest had enlisted the help of Lewis Galentiere, a friend from his Paris days and now a noted American translator, to correct the French, paying him with a small Spanish knife with a blade of Toledo steel for his help. "Wine of Wyoming" would be published in the August issue of *Scribner's Magazine*.

Even with a dry spell between checks, life was different from Ernest's poor days living in Paris on Hadley's puny trust fund, borrowing money from friends for train fare and bullfighting tickets. He didn't talk about it, but the truth was that he liked traveling in a certain style, driving new cars from Uncle Gus and ordering a custom Springfield rifle that he'd brought on this trip. Pauline had been raised in a family of good taste. She knew where to get the best of everything, and Uncle Gus was only too happy to help finance the lifestyle of his beloved niece and her husband. Gus had even enlisted the help of his pharmaceutical company in Spain to do research for Ernest's new nonfiction book about bullfighting: putting ads in newspapers to encourage their readers to share books, newspaper clippings, and mementos from bullfights.

The lifestyle Ernest appreciated—traveling to Paris, the bullfights in Pamplona, deep-sea fishing in Key West, and the Wyoming retreats—was expensive. Despite help from Pauline's wealthy family and robust sales from *A Farewell to Arms*, it was important to keep money flowing. But he couldn't accept magazine assignments when the new book demanded all his energy. The result was long periods where no money was coming in between his advance and actual sales of the book.

He planned to finish his bullfighting manuscript before leaving the ranch and return to Spain in the spring to gather more photos for the book. He imagined it to be a treatise on bullfighting and hoped to publish it the following year.

Ernest had left instructions to ship his trunk of bullfighting materials to his new address at the L Bar T Ranch. The only outside communication to the ranch was through cables sent to Cody, Wyoming, that were phoned to the Crandall Ranger Station fifteen miles away, and mail that came from Cooke City once a week.

THEN THERE WERE
THE DISTRACTIONS

ERNEST ATE HIS BREAKFAST at the lodge, keeping to himself. He felt he "couldn't learn anything from the dudes so there was no use talking to them." He always preferred talking with the wranglers.

Sometimes on his way back to the cabin, he'd stop at the corral, watching Ivan and another wrangler, Chub Weaver, saddle horses while Ernest sucked on a piece of hay. As he leaned on the fence, he took in the sounds—the jingling of tackle, the slap of a saddle, horses' snorting—and the scent of the barn—animal, hay, dust, and manure.

One day after breakfast, Ivan made the mistake of telling Ernest that the "fishing is going to be great."

"I've just got to work," Ernest replied. Lately the river had been churned up from cloudbursts, which helped him ignore the water's temptation. He kicked the dirt and then stormed to his cabin.

A few minutes later he returned to the corral. "Damn you, Ivan," he yelled. "You've ruined my whole day now . . . so let's go fishing."

Ernest used Hardy tackle, and his leaders, the length of line attached to the main line where flies are tied, were already made with three flies. His favorites were a McGinty for the top, Coch-y-Bondhu for the middle, and a woodcock green-and-yellow for the tail fly. Most of the time Ernest liked to fish across the river and cast downstream, as his flies skittered across the current. The Clarks Fork was still muddy, but Ernest caught ten cutthroats with a spinner on a fly.

FLAYING DEAD HORSES

AFTER THE DEATH of Ernest's father, Max Perkins had become a good friend, even visiting Ernest in Key West. When a package arrived from Max at the L Bar T on July 24—sent to Piggott after Ernest had already left for Wyoming—Ernest opened it and found a letter and a set of proofs for *In Our Time*.

Ernest responded to Max the same day, reminding him where to send the mail—delivered to the ranch once a week from Cooke City with telegrams sent to Lawrence Nordquist, Painter, Wyoming, where there was a ranger phone in that direction. He wanted Max to understand that sending him the *In Our Time* proofs was a great inconvenience and that Max was asking him to "stop and flay dead horses" instead of focusing on his new bullfighting book.

Max knew that Ernest needed all his creative juices to go into the bullfighting book and could barely write letters when he was concentrating on new work. Ernest had once told his parents that he was "as pleasant to be around as a bear with carbuncles" until a book was finished.

The book's title had been *in our time*—lowercase, following the modernist fashion in Paris to experiment with punctuation and capitalization—when it was published in 1924 by Three Mountains Press. And it had been well received after publication by its first American publisher Boni & Liveright in 1925. Ernest wrote the book in a style called "cablese," with vignettes inserted between chapters—little stories that sprang from the cables he had sent to the *Toronto Star* when he was a stringer in Paris, covering Europe. The cables required brief, succinct stories to save on per-word transmission costs. They were like snapshots, capturing a moment in time, that packed a punch.

Scribner's wanted to bring the book out again, adding an introduction by a critic, an author's note, and new material—and rearrange chapters. Ernest told Max he would work on *In Our Time* when work on the bullfighting book stalled, but until then he didn't want to switch gears.

It made him nervous. He worried there could be libel issues from some of the characters, especially from the story "Up in Michigan," because the reason the book seemed so true was because most of it was true. Ernest felt he hadn't had the skills back then, and perhaps still didn't, to change names and circumstances.

Ernest was against adding new material or changing the order of the chapters. "I want it to be the book as I wrote it and as it was intended to be published—That is its only value—I will not doctor it up for any other purpose." Ernest implored, "Max please believe me that those chapters are where they belong."

Ernest told Max he planned to stay on the ranch until the bullfighting book was done. He had already interrupted his work too much by traveling and he'd regained his focus, writing seven hundred to twelve hundred words a day, every day, since he arrived except one. "—This is a good place and not getting mail is a hell of a fine thing and very good for working," he wrote, signing the letter, "Yours always—Ernest—"

LETTERS FROM PIGGOTT

PAULINE RECEIVED A LETTER from her mother reporting on Patrick's good health and spirits; her family adored Patrick and enjoyed watching him grow. Her parents tried to be understanding of the nomadic life that she and Ernest led, with their transcontinental travel, Paris apartment, and leaving Patrick for months at a time in the care of others. Although Arkansas was a long way from the bright lights of a big city, her parents were well-read, sophisticated people who accepted that the travel fueled their writer son-in-law's work. But when they heard the news that the Hemingways had returned to Key West in February and their grandson was not an ocean away, they were overjoyed. They hoped Pauline and Ernest would now stay in one place. Mary had told them, "Get a good strong anchor and sink it deep and stay put for a while."

They had put down an anchor in Key West, renting a charming home on Pearl Street that their friends Charles and Lorine Thompson had found for them and setting up their household. How wonderful to put their clothes in drawers instead of living out of a suitcase! Looking back on their European trip, from April 1929 to February of the current year, Pauline had realized the importance of taking time to recharge. It was easy for her to overexert herself, trying to keep up with Ernest.

Her health had deteriorated over time following their previous trip to Wyoming in 1928. Pauline had given birth to Patrick by caesarean section in June, come to Wyoming for hunting and fishing with Ernest in August, returned briefly to Piggott in September, and then headed on a tour of the East Coast in October, a whirlwind of parties and football games and visiting friends. She and Ernest had visited Ada and Archie MacLeish, Scott and Zelda Fitzgerald, and Gaylord Donnelley from Folly Ranch. Ernest had been in a celebratory mode after finishing the draft of *A Farewell to Arms* at Spear-O-Wigwam—who was she to hold him back?

The party ended on December 6 with news that Ernest's father had died. Pauline had gone into a protective mode of Ernest, taking charge of their household. The holiday month turned into a month of mourning as Ernest helped his mother, and Pauline made certain a comfortable home awaited him when he returned to Key West.

Ernest had poured himself into *A Farewell to Arms* revisions with Sunny, who had come to live with them in the fall, taking shifts with Pauline to type the manuscript. After completing the book on January 22, 1929, Ernest invited Max to come to Key West to pick it up and enjoy some deep-sea fishing. Other friends who visited were Waldo Peirce, Katy Smith, and John Dos Passos—a continuous party.

Their household had expanded from just the two of them to five people to feed and care for. Despite Sunny's help with Patrick and the manuscript, Pauline was stretched with needs from a demanding husband, an infant, an active five-year-old stepson, her sister-in-law, and an endless stream of guests. When their family entourage left Havana Harbor aboard the *Yorck*, bound for Boulogne, on April 5, 1929, Pauline had become extremely ill. The frenetic pace from the past year had finally caught up with her.

On the ship, Sunny stayed in a cabin with Patrick and Bumby to take care of them while Pauline slept all day, rallying only at night to accompany Ernest to dinner and drinks with new friends he had met. She knew better than to leave him alone, with so many women on the ship who would happily keep him company. Upon arrival in Paris, the doctor diagnosed her with exhaustion and a sinus infection so severe that she had to have her sinuses drained at the hospital twice.

Things got worse in Paris when she and Patrick both got the grippe and she couldn't get out of bed. She knew Ernest was not good around sick people, that he couldn't care for them. He had left them alone at the apartment, traveling south to Hendaye, Spain, to work on the revisions to *A Farewell to Arms* requested by Scribner's, leaving them on their own to recover.

When Pauline was a child, she would become delirious with just a slight fever, and her parents still worried about her. Her mother had recommended turning the children and household over to Virginia (Jinny) and going away to get some rest, because if Pauline lost her health, her life would be miserable.

It took months to get her strength back, and she still hadn't felt up to attending the bullfights in Pamplona in July with Ernest, so he went instead with Jinny and Guy Hickok. Pauline agreed to meet him after the festival, when she was feeling stronger. She made arrangements to send Patrick to Bordeaux with his new French nurse, Henriette, for two months, but before leaving Paris, Pauline took care to catch up on the chores she'd neglected while she was ill—mending Ernest's clothes, paying bills, and purchasing items that Ernest had requested.

The weather in Spain was glorious—sunny and warm—and she wrote to Jinny that they were having a fine time "swimming and loafing." With the revisions to *A Farewell to Arms* finished, Ernest was between books—and, as he often was before starting another project, he was moody. Pauline knew it had nothing to do with her; she took it in stride.

After being away from the United States for nearly a year, Ernest, Pauline, and Patrick returned to Key West with Henriette in February 1930. (Sunny had returned to Oak Park earlier, after touring Europe with a friend.) Pauline had her health back, and they were happy in Florida until the heat came and Ernest wanted to return to Wyoming's cooler climates.

Being at the ranch provided a reprieve from Pauline's duties as a toddler's mother, plus she got a break from cooking, cleaning, and managing a household. Pulling on her jeans and boots and adding a fishing vest and her black cap, she headed out on an adventure with the other guests and guides. When Ernest was ready for a break, she'd have a picnic waiting and horses saddled to explore fishing holes several miles downstream, just the two of them. Pure heaven.

Pauline wearing her "wedding pants" in a stream. *Ernest Hemingway Collection, John F. Kennedy Presidential Library and Museum, Boston*

JACK AT THE RANCH

JACK HAD FINISHED HIS CHORES—starting the fire with soaked sawdust and a few small logs—so he was free to meet his new best friend, Billy Sidley, at the corral. Billy's family was from Chicago, and they'd been coming to the ranch for several summers—they even built their own log cabin at the ranch, and Billy's grandpa's ashes were scattered on a mountaintop here. Ivan made sure all the children had properly fitting saddles, and he had taught them to saddle up by themselves. Jack and Billy, decked out in chaps and cowboy hats, imagined themselves as real horse wranglers.

Jack's horse, Pinky, was an extremely clever animal. When Jack cinched the saddle tight, the way Ivan had shown him, Pinky would bloat up his stomach with air. After Jack was on the saddle, Pinky would release the air and the saddle would loosen and slip, causing Jack many accidents. Jack learned to tap Pinky on the ribs right before cinching, startling him into releasing the air, and Jack quickly tightened the cinch like a professional.

While adults went off on their own rides, the wranglers took the children to lakes and streams or up the Squaw Trail into Hurricane Mesa country. Some days, the kids would play horseback tag in the pasture, and at the end of the game, the horses were tired, ready to get to the barn, where their saddles would be removed and they'd get a good brushing. One day Jack forgot something at the cabin, so he decided to ride Pinky over to the cabin before taking him back to the barn, but Pinky didn't like that idea. Wanting to go with the other horses, he didn't budge. Jack resorted to giving Pinky the leather quirt and Pinky bolted, running full speed ahead through the cabins, where Olive Nordquist had stretched wire laundry lines through pine trees. Jack dodged the first wire, but the next one caught him across the chest and knocked him out of the saddle. Luckily, he wasn't seriously injured. After that, Jack was more cautious about using the leather quirt.

On days that Pauline went out with her own guides, Jack would hang back, waiting for the opportunity to go fishing with his dad. He desperately wanted to learn, and he hoped one day his father would take him along. When an invitation didn't come, and he saw Ernest take off alone with his fishing gear, Jack took matters into his own hands and followed him. He found Ernest chest-deep in the water and hid in the shadows to watch his dad fish, unnoticed.

Apparently Jack wasn't as stealthy as he'd imagined, because Ernest walked over to the bank. "You know, Schatz, trout spook awfully easily—" (Ernest's other nickname for Bumby was "Schatz.")

"I'm sorry, Papa, I only wanted—"

"If you really want to watch just stay back a little from the bank. You mustn't move around until I go further down. Then move very slowly and stay low," Ernest instructed.

"Yes Papa!" Jack was delighted that he hadn't been sent back to the ranch.

"That way the trout won't spook."

Jack sat quietly by the stream, watching his father fish and nearly dying with impatience. In France, Jack had caught his first fish in a gentle little river with a hook made from a safety pin, a line from strong black thread, and a willow shoot for a rod. Bait was rolled-up balls of dough that the cook had given him. He watched minnows in the crystal-clear water and dangled the bait until he felt a tug and pulled out a shiny minnow. It was thrilling as the minnow flopped on the dock. He caught minnow after minnow, using his pockets as a creel and bringing them back to the cook, who fried them for his supper. But the trout that Papa caught "were so beautiful," Jack became obsessed with catching one himself.

BIOGRAPHICAL CRAP

THE WEEKLY MAIL ARRIVED, and in it, a copy of a new Grosset & Dunlap edition of *The Sun Also Rises*. When Ernest turned it over and read the book jacket copy, he nearly blew a gasket. Soon after, he wrote to Max asking him to tell G. and D. "to at once remove that biographical crap [underlined three times] i.e. SHIT about me on the back wrapper explaining to G. and D. what my position is about personal publicity."

Early in their relationship, Ernest had told Max he was very sensitive about personal publicity and said any biographical material that Scribner's put out about him ought to be true. He had even written his mother after publication of *A Farewell to Arms*, asking her to tell reporters she had promised not to answer questions about him because Ernest wanted to keep his private life out of the press.

So how had this happened? He'd never approved this jacket copy. He didn't know who'd given the publisher the information, but if Grosset & Dunlap didn't remove all personal information about his war service, his marriage, and his private life, he would never publish another book with them. "So HeLp Me GoD," he wrote. "I tell you *[EH insertion: (this sort of thing)]* it takes any possible pleasure out of writing."

It was a reminder of the lesson Ernest had learned early in his career, when someone had circulated false information about his service in Italy: people thought *he* was the one telling the lies about his record. That's when he learned that he needed to control his publicity. In fact, going forward he would create the public persona that he wanted; he would decide what the world would be allowed to see. When Max's cable arrived a few days later, telling him that all the book jackets would be destroyed and no copies had yet been sold, or would be sold, with the offending cover, Ernest was still sore but had calmed down slightly. He sent Max a cable to thank him for his help.

VIVE LA MARRIAGE

AT FOLLY RANCH TWO YEARS EARLIER, one of the girls had captured longtime bachelor Bill Horne's interest. Bill and Frances "Bunny" Thorne were married on August 21, 1929, at Folly Ranch, and they sent Ernest and Pauline a telegram in Santiago, Spain, telling them the news. Ernest couldn't have been happier. Their friends John Dos Passos and Katy Smith had also recently married.

Ernest had witnessed Cupid's arrow striking both couples—Bill and Bunny in Wyoming and Dos and Katy in Key West. When Dos and Katy had visited at the same time last spring, Dos was smitten, later saying "from the first moment I couldn't think of anything but her green eyes."

Ernest believed in marriage. A man needed a woman by his side and in his bed. After a day's work, it was wonderful to be with your wife— even though things had become complicated since Patrick's birth and the doctor's warning that Pauline could not give birth again for three years without literally risking her life. Her Catholic beliefs prohibited birth control, so they followed a strict sexual regimen of careful scheduling and coitus interruptus.

Physical activity was something that helped distract Ernest, and Pauline wasn't like other wives, instead accepting his need for male company and adventure. When Ernest had been stranded for twelve days with Mike Strater, Archie MacLeish, John Hermann, and Captain Burge Saunders in the Dry Tortugas in the spring of 1929, and were finally rescued by an American yacht, Pauline hadn't worried. Ernest felt that was a good trait in a woman.

Ernest had invited the Hornes to join them at the L Bar T this summer, sharing half their cabin, and Bill had responded, "Sure we are going with you if that's jake with you—gosh!" Ernest knew that Bunny was an intrepid adventurer; at Folly she'd slept on the ground in tents and had ridden on the ten-day pack trip in the Wyoming backcountry. The newlyweds planned to arrive August 8 and stay for two weeks.

Ernest wrote to "Orny" telling him not to worry about leaders—Ernest had plenty—and he also had a couple of rods they were welcome to borrow. But in case Bill wanted to buy a rod, Ernest enclosed a page torn from a catalog with a couple recommendations circled, saying it all depended on whether Bill wanted to spend the jack.

He also asked if Bill would be bringing whiskey. If not, they could buy it at the ranch, which had bootlegger connections in Red Lodge. And wouldn't it be great to be sitting on the porch drinking a cocktail after a fine day in the forest or the river? Ernest closed by giving the old "Article" his best, and sent love to Bunny from Pauline and him, signing the letter "Steen," short for one of his nicknames, "Hemingsteen."

LIBEL ACTION

ERNEST TOOK TIME OUT of his writing schedule, something he was loath to do, to review the proofs for *In Our Time*, and he still found problems with Scribner's plan to reissue the book. Ernest wrote to Max, telling him his concerns. He had tried rewriting "Up in Michigan" to keep it from being libelous, but it took all the story's character away. Yet to publish it as it currently was could lead to a lawsuit from the real people depicted as characters in the story. The book would need to include a disclaimer that this story was not based on any living person.

The next matter was the book's introduction, which the publisher insisted on adding. Ernest suggested that the critic Edmund "Bunny" Wilson write it. Although Ernest despised most critics, he had appreciated Wilson's review of *The Sun Also Rises* and thought Wilson seemed decent enough. Ernest felt that *In Our Time* was a hell of a good book—it had been his first book and had a limited distribution in Paris, and he liked the idea of making it available to people who had read his other work. With a good introduction and a disclaimer, it should be ready.

Before ending his letter to Max, he reported that he'd worked six days every week on his new bullfighting book and had written sixty thousand words. Also, he had six cases of beer—enough to finish six more chapters. Ernest told Max he was sorry for sounding rude and that Max should not take it personally. It was just that when he was working hard and received a letter about a problem, it interrupted his concentration.

THE MAN WHO INVENTED
MONTANA

BUNNY AND BILL took the train from Chicago, then boarded a bus and rode across the east half of Yellowstone National Park to Cooke City, Montana, arriving on August 8. A group of riders met them with mounts, and Ernest rode up on a big steed, "straight legged, Indian-fashion because of his gimpy knee" from his war injuries. According to Bill, "He looked like the man who invented Montana."

The group rode nine miles south down a valley, past Index and Pilot Peaks, to where the land rose above Clarks Fork into steep hills with narrow stretches of forest. In the distance, they saw ridges of Beartooth Buttes, fifteen miles to the east. It was just before dusk when the group got to the ranch.

The Hornes had arrived during a rainy spell; it had been raining for days, with cloudbursts putting the river "on the bum," for a week—the trout hid behind the rocks. Pauline entertained the couple with other activities until the streams cleared, while Ernest continued to work on his book and correspond with Max about *In Our Time.*

When the rain finally stopped, the fishing was glorious; Bill had never met such trout fishing. The fish were so hungry that many times the fishing party hooked two on at once, and occasionally three. The group caught more than a hundred fish. Most were returned to the stream, but some were eaten at dinner at the ranch house, or for breakfast in the cabin, with Ernest cooking them with salt, pepper, and lemon on the little stove.

Bill admired Ernest's dedication to writing the new bullfighting book. One day they had been at a spot where "the river was about to dive down into a canyon and become inaccessible. It was fast, beautiful water full of trout, the kind of thing an avid fisherman would sell his soul for." Yet while the group fished, "Ernest sat in the sun in an old rocker reading about Corridas." Ernest's trunk of Spanish bullfighting periodicals and books from Uncle Gus, along with materials Ernest had collected on his trips to Spain, had arrived.

One day, when fishing hadn't been good, Ernest had taken Bill on an adventure to check on bear bait that he and Ivan Wallace had set to catch a bear in the valley. Ranchers had complained that a bear had been coming down from the mountains and eating their cattle.

Ernest told Bill that he and Ivan had ridden up Index Peak to search for the perfect spot for the bait. They found a clearing along a fast-moving stream that would take a grizzly more than a few seconds to cross. Rocks and trees created a natural blind and offered hiding places for the men as they waited for the bear. For bait, they had shot a horse and set fire to it, creating a terrible stench. When the horse was cooked about halfway, they put out the fire and rode back to the ranch. It would take about a week for grizzlies to discover the carcass and watch it, making sure there weren't hunters nearby, before they feasted on it.

Bill rode up with Ernest to check on it, but the bait was still intact.

THE COW-EATING BEAR

AUGUST WAS AN UNUSUAL TIME of year for a bear to come down from the mountains and kill cattle—twenty head had been lost. The ranchers wanted it stopped, and recognized it was a job for a professional; that's why they'd hired Ivan Wallace. In addition to being the L Bar T wrangler, Ivan was a well-respected hunter and trapper, so they enlisted him to set the bait for the bear on Index Peak.

The day after Bill and Bunny returned home to Chicago, Ernest gladly paused work on his bullfighting book to ride with Ivan up Index Peak to check on the bait again. His horse Goofy was loaded down with food, raincoats, binoculars, and Ernest's precious new Springfield rifle, strapped in a scabbard.

One lucky day the previous year he'd been in the elevator of Abercrombie & Fitch in New York City when he ran into Milford Baker, a buddy from his Italian Red Cross ambulance driver days. They reconnected over their love of guns, and Milford turned out to be extremely knowledgeable—he offered to help Ernest order a custom-made Springfield rifle. They had written nine letters back and forth about the gun, with many personal details and measurements going into making it the perfect gun for Ernest, and in June, six months later, Ernest received it, calling it an absolutely splendid rifle. It was love at first sight.

Ernest bragged to friends that it was the most beautiful gun he'd ever seen and that it didn't have a kick. He sounded like a Springfield advertisement, saying he'd never seen a classier gun in his life and it could be used for "everything but shooting elephants." He would need to order another gun to take with him on safari in Africa for those conditions.

The only thing was its weight. At nine pounds it was too heavy to lug up a mountain. Ernest had spotted bighorn sheep on the mountainside with a scope from the ranch as he awaited the season opening on September 15 and wrote to Milford about ordering another lighter gun, perhaps a 6.5-mm Mannlicher, to use when he climbed. Would it be possible to get it in time for bighorn sheep season? In the meantime, he'd bring the Springfield on his saddle to hunt bears.

As Ivan and Ernest made their way up the mountain, something spooked Goofy; the horse bolted into the dense forest with Ernest holding on for dear life, afraid to bail off the horse in "fear of busting or losing" his gun. He stayed on the mare too long, and a sharp tree branch sliced his chin below the lip. Luckily the gun survived without damage, but Ernest didn't fare as well, with a gash that wouldn't stop bleeding. The men headed down the mountain to get Ernest to the doctor.

They rode to the Crandall Ranger Station, where the forest ranger agreed to have his daughter Velma Williams drive them to a doctor in Cody. The road was more of a mule trail than a passage for cars—narrow, steep, and winding as it traversed Sunlight Basin and Dead Indian Pass. It took them three hours to reach town, and they arrived at midnight.

Cody, Wyoming, was a Wild West outpost, the creation of Buffalo Bill Cody in 1896. Recognizing the money to be made, Cody had sat on a hill and seen the perfect spot for a new town that the railroad could go through, taking passengers to Yellowstone. When Ernest and Ivan rolled into town, the only doctor they could locate, Dr. Trueblood, was a veterinarian turned physician. He wanted to knock Ernest out with anesthesia before suturing the wound, but Ernest wouldn't have that; he insisted on using whiskey for an anesthetic.

Rejecting the doctor's offer of bootleg whiskey, Ernest convinced him to write a prescription for two bottles of Old Oscar Pepper, a Kentucky bourbon that during Prohibition was available only for medicinal purposes. After Ernest was stitched back up, the ranger's daughter drove, while the two men drank Ernest's medicine. She had to regularly stop to open and pass through cattle gates, and at each of these stops Ernest and Ivan would take another pull from the Old Oscar Pepper, feeling no pain by the time they arrived back at the ranch.

The *Cody Enterprise* ran a story about his visit:

> Ernest Hemingway was brought to Cody on Tuesday evening to receive surgical attention caused by an accident that afternoon when a horse bolted with him, carrying him through some heavy brush and tearing his face in such a manner as to require several stitches to patch up the wounds. Mr. Hemingway is a prominent author and writer of Chicago and Paris. He was driven to town by Miss Velma Williams.

––––––––––––

The men slept off their bender, arising late the next morning and heading back up to the bear bait, hiding in the nearby blind. Ernest told Ivan stories as they waited—about Italy and driving an ambulance in the Great War, about the bombs exploding and the mud splashing him in the face, and about the nurse he met after he was wounded and how they fell in love—stories that he'd included in his book *A Farewell to Arms*.

"I haven't read any of your books," Ivan told Ernest.

"We get along pretty good—and by not reading anything I wrote, we can keep it that way," Ernest replied.

Their conversations would be followed by long periods of silence when Ernest would scratch notes into the tablet he'd brought along to capture the sights and sounds of the land.

Just after sunset, as Ernest watched the bait, a brown-colored black bear ambled out of the woods to feed on the carcass. Ernest's heart was pounding when he shot the old male from eighty-five yards. It was so dark he could hardly see. He killed the bear with two shots: the first shot, through the ribs, knocked it down and the second, through the shoulder, killed it instantly. It was Ernest's first bear.

The next day, upon returning to the L Bar T, Ernest approached Lawrence Nordquist about buying Goofy.

"If you want a good saddle horse, I can supply a much better one," Lawrence said.

"I don't want to ride him," Ernest said. "I want to shoot him for bear bait."

Sparing Goofy, at least for a time, Ernest shot a second bear on August 30 from one hundred yards, killing it instantly with a bullet through the neck.

Ernest's chin hadn't healed properly, so he had to return to Cody to have it restitched. Before leaving, he stopped at the corral and ripped two long strings of hair from Goofy's hide. When he arrived at the doctor's office, he told him he'd like his chin sewn up with the horse hair.

BIG GAME HUNTER

IN EARLY SEPTEMBER there was snow on the hills when Ernest implored his friends Mike Strater and Archie MacLeish to come to the L Bar T and hunt with him. Pauline and Jack would be leaving on September 13 for Jack's return to Paris at the start of the school year; Ernest would be alone on the ranch through October. His letters sounded like missives from the Wyoming Tourism Board, guaranteeing they'd get shots at elk, deer, and bighorn sheep, in addition to the world-class rainbow trout fishing. Lawrence Nordquist charged twenty-five dollars a day to guide two people into the backcountry, and a sixty-dollar license allowed for one elk, one deer, bear, game birds, and loads of trout. A license for bighorn sheep cost fifteen dollars extra.

Ernest planned to go to Africa in the spring, financed by Uncle Gus, who'd offered to stake Ernest and three friends. The two men had hatched the idea when they'd traveled together to Berlin last year. Ernest had invited Charles Thompson, Mike Strater, and Archie MacLeish to join him on safari.

As he lauded Wyoming's beautiful country, he also told his friends that it was home to the only dangerous animal in North America—the grizzly—and shooting it would be great training for Africa.

Ernest was also still arguing with Max, who didn't seem to understand how to get mail to him, over the publication of *In Our Time*. On September 3 he received a letter from Max dated August 18. It had been delayed because it had been sent to Painter instead of Cooke City, despite

Ernest's instruction about where to send his mail. Max was still stuck on the subject of additional material for the new printing.

Ernest replied that he felt he had accommodated Max's wish by including a revised version of "Mr. and Mrs. Elliot," originally titled "Mr. and Mrs. Smith,"* which Pauline was currently typing, and he promised to send Max the manuscript the next day if possible. But he didn't see how he could put in additional material. Plus, he was still worried about libel.

He set the letter aside that morning and came back to it later, writing in black ink. He hadn't had trouble with libel when the book was previously published, but its press run had been limited. In his view, it just wasn't worth the risk; if Scribner's must bring it out again, they do so at their own risk. This book was interrupting his focus on his bullfighting book, and it was all "skinning dead horses" to him.

Another concern about the "additional material" Scribner's was asking for: Ernest did not want to trick readers into thinking they were buying a book with new material by the author when they were not. And he had recommended Bunny Wilson to write the introduction if there really needed to be an introduction, and Max still hadn't told him if Wilson had agreed.

That night, before sending the letter, Ernest added more thoughts in pencil around the left, top, and right margins, like little animal tracks around a watering hole. He admitted to Max that he was "smashed up" from an accident, with a six-inch gash in his jaw. Still, Ernest wrote, he'd never been healthier or in better shape in his life.

---

* "Mr. and Mrs. Elliot" was restored to its original form as it appeared in the Autumn–Winter 1924–1925 Little Review. *Letters, Vol. 4,* 357n2.

GIRL FRIDAY

PAULINE WAS WRAPPING UP her last two weeks at the ranch as she typed up Ernest's short story "Mr. and Mrs. Elliot." It had been a wonderful summer, with time for herself when she wasn't acting as Ernest's editor and secretary. However, Jack needed to get back home to Paris for school, so they would soon need to return to Piggott to pick up Henriette and then continue to New York, where Henriette and Jack would board the ship.

Pauline would see Patrick only briefly while in Piggott, but after she dropped off Jack and Henriette, she'd return and become reacquainted with her son while they waited for Ernest to pick them up on the first of November. She looked forward to going back to Key West for some happy home life this winter.

Pauline had signed up for a marriage where Ernest's needs came first, and he expected her to be with him. There were times she had to choose between being a mother or a wife, something her family didn't understand.

But as much as Ernest sometimes acted like a disinterested father, Pauline had observed a touching scene one night while they sat at the lodge with a group of friends at Jack's bedtime. It was dark outside, and their cabin was the farthest from the lodge. Everyone knew Jack was afraid to cross the ranch alone at night, but they didn't want to embarrass him. All of a sudden Ernest jumped up.

"Damn," he said. "I forgot something at the cabin. I'll have to walk back with you, Bumby."

At the ranch, as Pauline made preparations to leave, she felt it was time for her and Ernest to update their wills. They had become friends with the Sidleys—Jack's friend Billy's parents—and William Pratt Sidley happened to be a Chicago lawyer. The will was witnessed by his wife, Elaine Dupee Sidley, and Lawrence Nordquist on September 13, 1930, naming William P. Sidley as Pauline's successor if she was unable to act as executrix. Before she left the ranch, they signed their new wills, leaving everything to each other, and then to the two boys.

Surely the need she had felt to update their wills was nothing more than being responsible parents. But the women in her family had been known to have "the gift," possessing clairvoyant powers, and once, in Paris, Pauline had demonstrated hers. She and Ernest had been sitting at a café and when a man walked up to their table, she had blurted out, "You're dead!" startling the man. Later that same day while crossing the street, he was hit by a car and died. Was the need she felt to write their wills a premonition?

She would be saying goodbye to Ernest for over a month while he stayed at the ranch to hunt. At least while she was away, she wouldn't worry about him getting in trouble at the secluded ranch miles away from civilization.

HIS TURN

Jack had watched his father all summer from the sidelines, learning about casting and playing fish—not rushing a fish but not playing it too long either. He'd learned how to clean fish, and to place fish in a creel on fresh leaves, keeping them damp and cool. He'd even learned how to cook a fish; his father suggested leaving the lungs inside for better flavor and cooking it with salt, pepper, and lemon. But he still hadn't actually gone fishing. Jack could hardly wait for his turn to throw a line in the water. He was determined to catch a real fish.

On one of their last days on the ranch, Pauline invited Jack to go fishing with her outfit. He was given a rod with a six-foot leader and a grasshopper for bait. He had cast the wriggling grasshopper in the swirling back eddies and was waiting to see what happened when the line was suddenly pulled underwater. He felt a tug and gave a strong yank—his rod bent, and he felt a fish fighting to get away. Using the skills he'd observed while watching his father, Jack miraculously landed an eleven-inch rainbow cutthroat. It looked enormous compared to the minnows he'd caught in France, a reward for his patience all summer.

He ate every bit of his fish for supper at the ranch house that night amid much fuss. It was the perfect way to end his summer at the L Bar T, and it planted the seed for his obsession to become a fly-fisherman.

SNOW LIKE CHRISTMAS MORNING

ERNEST AND LAWRENCE NORDQUIST headed into the high mountains during a snowstorm, a two-day ride ahead of them to reach their hunting territory. High above the timber, on their first day of hunting, Ernest spied a group of sheep above timberline through the binoculars—standing out as four white spots due to the coloring on their rumps. The country was rough and rocky, the wind blew in hellacious gales, and there was nowhere to take cover.

To reach the herd, Ernest hiked around the mountain peak, then crawled on his belly to get a closer look. The group included an old ram with a beautiful head, and when Ernest was close enough for a good shot, he fired, dropping the ram to the ground.

The other sheep seemed puzzled, not understanding what had happened, and came over to see why the old ram wasn't running. They stayed there near him, not sure what to do, since their boss wasn't moving. Ernest could have shot all three.

From the size of the ram's horns, Ernest and Lawrence estimated it to be thirteen years old, very old for a sheep. They butchered him and appreciated his fine trophy head.

With the sheep bagged, the men headed lower on the mountain to hunt elk in thick timber. The elk weren't bugling yet, so it was hard to find them, but finally one afternoon they came across a bull and twelve cows hiding in the dense forest. When the herd emerged from the trees,

Ernest shot the bull with six points on each of its antlers, another fine trophy mount. He planned to send some of the elk meat to Bunny and Bill Horne if the weather stayed cold enough to ship it.

Ernest had ordered the 6.5-mm Mannlicher rifle with Milford Baker's help, but it didn't arrive before he left for camp. One day, one of the ranch hands made the two-day ride up to the camp to deliver Ernest's new gun to him along with his mail. Although Ernest had already taken his ram, he was delighted to get the new gun and do some practice shooting at a blue jay and a camp robber high in the top of a spruce.* The gun was very handsome, and it shot beautifully with both iron sights and scope.

It had been a successful hunt, and Ernest thought this country was wonderful. Game hunting was some of the best fun he had ever had. By the time he and Lawrence rode back to the ranch on September 28, they had spotted two grizzlies, a gray wolf, and two eagles.

---

* Camp robbers are several species of jays known for their fearlessness around humans to steal food from camps.

MAIL CALL

WHEN ERNEST RETURNED to the L Bar T, a stack of mail was waiting for him, including several letters and a wire from Max. It seemed that Max had sent the wire—and the mail—to the wrong address again. It must seem impossible for someone in New York City to understand that mail was only delivered once a week, shuttled from a town fourteen miles away. Although Ernest enjoyed the solitary life on the ranch without much communication to the outside world, it did add an extra layer of complications when there were weeklong lags between letters, and Max was trying to get Ernest's book ready to go to the printer on October 24.

Ernest was happy to learn from Max, at last, that Bunny Wilson had agreed to write the introduction for *In Our Time*. In his response to Max, Ernest inquired about the dramatization of *A Farewell to Arms*. After selling the rights, Ernest hadn't heard a word about the play. Had it been successful on Broadway? He told Max to let him know what had happened to the play.

He was on page 200 of the bullfighting book, he wrote, but he needed to go to Spain for the illustrations; unless he stopped in Spain en route to Africa next spring, the book might not be ready to bring out in 1931. Ernest hoped to have the first draft written by Christmas, and he thought it would be a damned fine book. He signed off, "Best to you always—Ernest."

ON STAGE AND SCREEN

ERNEST HADN'T HEARD from Pauline since she left Piggott for New York with Jack and Henriette on September 27. He wrote to Archie on October 6, and again on October 12, wondering if Archie might have seen her when she was in New York taking Jack to the ship.

At last, news about the play arrived, but it hadn't come from Max—it came from Milford Baker, who told him he had seen the play, and it had been "an awful mess." Ernest thanked Milford for being so frank and explained that he hadn't been involved in the production; his agent had sold the rights and he hadn't even read the script.

Despite the bad news about the play, good news arrived that Paramount was offering $80,000 to purchase the film rights for *A Farewell to Arms*. Matthew Herold, Pauline's cousin (and former fiancé) and also the Hemingways' attorney, was working on the legal details and sent Ernest a contract to sign and have notarized. Ernest explained there was not a notary anywhere near the ranch, and due to two weeks of rain the road was now impassable. He strongly urged that Paramount would need to accept his power of attorney signature.

After commissions to his agent and the producers, Ernest would get a cut of about $26,000—money he planned to start saving for his *own* family. His mother seemed to think he was made of money—she mistakenly thought he was getting rich from the Broadway play—and that he should be sending her more to help out. But he made clear it was time for him to start thinking of his family's future.

Ernest caught up on correspondence and worked on his book as he waited for the next hunting trip, this time with John Dos Passos. Ernest had written to Dos shortly after arriving at the ranch, extolling the virtues of the wild Wyoming country he'd discovered. When he made a new discovery about a new sport or a new place, he became evangelical, spreading the word. And, after all, Dos originally introduced Ernest to Key West.

Good ol' Dos had agreed to take the train out West and go hunting with Ernest in the high country. Although he couldn't see worth a damn and was not in good physical shape, Dos was always willing for an adventure. Dos would arrive in mid-October and meet Ernest for the end of hunting season.

DOS PASSOS
IN THE HIGH COUNTRY

WHILE HIS WIFE, Katy, stayed with relatives, Dos traveled to Billings, Montana, on October 21, 1930, where Ernest met him at the train. Dos wasn't surprised to see a new scar on Ernest's face in addition to the horseshoe-shaped scar on his forehead. He knew that as much as Ernest was a tough guy, he was also accident prone.

Although Dos was not a natural athlete like Ernest, or a hunter, he was happy to accompany his friend in a land he'd never seen before. They left the ranch on pack mules, flanking the edge of Yellowstone National Park. The elk, with their keen sense of smell, kept getting wind of the men and bolting into the park, where they were safe.

Unable to shoot well because of his nearsightedness, Dos occupied himself by taking in the scenery—bears, beavers in a pond—while "watching Hem as a hunter." Ernest could almost smell an elk before the elk smelled him. And he understood the topography like a great military tactician, knowing what land in the next valley would be like before his horse made his way to the top of the rim rock.

The hills were dotted with illegal stills, and mules were used to lug the illicit hooch from Montana into Wyoming, so the men did not lack for booze. They feasted on venison and elk steaks washed down with bootleg wine and whiskey hauled from Red Lodge through the Beartooth Gap.

On October 28 they rode forty miles back to the ranch to start packing for the trip back home. Their route would take them to Billings, where Ernest would drop Dos at the train, before continuing to Sheridan, Kansas City, and Piggott. A wrangler at the ranch, Floyd Allington, was going to join them, heading back to Florida with Ernest to do some fishing.

LEAVE-TAKING

ERNEST TACKLED HIS PILE of mail before leaving the ranch, writing letters to Max, fellow writer Ford Madox Ford, translator Samuel Putnam, *Cosmopolitan* magazine editor Ray Long, and Caresse Crosby, who with her husband Harry had published some of Ernest's early works in Paris through their Black Sun Press.

Although the country was beautiful in the fall, winter would be coming soon and it was time to leave. He had logged ninety-two trout and shot two bears, a bull elk, and the old ram. He was on page 280, nearly done with his book, with plans to finish the last two chapters and the four appendices by Christmas.

On October 31 he packed up the Ford with fishing gear, rifles, sleeping bags, and a bottle of bootleg bourbon and headed out. Ernest was the driver, with Dos in the front seat and Floyd in the rumble seat. They spent the first night camping at Mammoth Hot Springs in Yellowstone, got up, shook the frost off their sleeping bags, and then set off for Billings.

It was just after sundown near Billings, and Ernest was driving when suddenly an oncoming car pulled out of its lane to pass without enough room. Ernest swerved to avoid a collision, rolling the roadster in a ditch. Floyd and Dos managed to climb out of the wreckage and extracted Ernest, who was pinned behind the wheel, his right arm badly injured. The men flagged down a passing motorist, who gave them a ride to Saint Vincent Hospital in Billings.

ADMITTANCE CLERK

WHEN THREE SCRUFFY-LOOKING MEN in dirty dungarees came into Saint Vincent's emergency room, the admittance nurse sized them up as cowboys.

"Occupation?" she asked as she filled out paperwork.

Ernest, in pain, clenched his shirt cuff in his teeth in an attempt to support his injured arm, mumbling when he spoke. "Writer," Ernest said.

She wrote "rider," as in bronc or bull rider.

Dos was uninjured, but Floyd had suffered a dislocated shoulder and Ernest's right arm was badly broken, an oblique spiral fracture above his elbow. He was admitted into the hospital for surgery, but it wasn't until the next day that the doctor came in to check on the patient and recognized Ernest Hemingway the *writer*, not rider.

It may have been headlights blinding Ernest that caused the accident, or it may have been the sun setting and the light hitting him right in the eyes—or, as Dos mentioned, it may have been the bootleg bourbon they'd been drinking. (Since they didn't want trouble over the illegal bourbon, they had quickly disposed of the evidence.) Dos telegraphed Pauline in Arkansas about the accident, and she boarded the next train to Billings.

SOS MAX

PLEASE FORWARD ALL MAIL FOR TEN DAYS SAINTVINCENTS HOSPITAL BIL-
LINGS MONTANA GETTING ALONG ALL RIGHT MAY BE HERE THREE WEEKS =
ERNEST.

PAULINE TAKES DICTATION

PAULINE HAD BARELY returned from New York to Piggott when Dos's telegram came. She went into action, arranging for Patrick to continue to stay with her family while she caught the next train to Billings. Dos met her at the depot in the repaired Ford—it had received only minor damage when it flipped, with two sprung doors and some scratches. When she arrived at Ernest's room, she found him heavily sedated with morphine and in great pain. But he would live, thank God. There was no need right now for the wills they had drawn up at the Nordquist Ranch.

After four days of unsuccessful attempts to maneuver the bones back into place, Ernest's physician, Dr. Louis Allard, determined that Ernest needed surgery. Ernest's luck prevailed when he got Dr. Allard for his doctor—Allard was a nationally known expert on orthopedic surgery.

On November 6, Dr. Allard operated on Ernest for two hours, setting his arm three times. Allard notched the bone, boring a hole through one side, then tied it together with kangaroo tendons. When Ernest heard about the kangaroo tendons, he made many jokes to his friends about his boxing ability improving.

He was required to keep his arm immobilized for the next couple weeks, and Pauline stayed by his side, attending to his needs, trying to make him comfortable. It was hard on her to see him in such pain.

When Ernest started feeling better, he wanted to catch up on correspondence, so Pauline rented a three-dollar-a-month noiseless typewriter and took dictation—something Ernest wasn't used to and didn't enjoy, preferring to write his own letters. For now it was the only option he had. Jacked up on morphine, he dictated a letter to Mike Strater.

He explained to Mike about his current condition, and that Pauline was doing fine and was typing the letter. She was finding the correspondence somewhat interesting until he got on the subject of guns. Pauline typed pages as Ernest expounded on the type of guns they would need for their African safari. Apparently, Charles Thompson had received a gun he'd also ordered from Milford Baker, but his gun wasn't sighted properly, and Ernest warned Mike not to judge a gun until it has been properly sighted. He reminded Mike that a man shoots best after practicing; it was like hours in the air, or the number of tarpon caught, or anything like that. Confidence at close range only comes with lots of shooting. Ernest recommended the merits of the old .30-30 Winchester for quick running shots and the lighter 6.5-mm Mannlicher for long-range shots. He continued by sharing a recap of his own shooting experience at the ranch with the Springfield and the Mannlicher, which had no kick. He'd shot the heads off numerous grouse. Ernest hoped the accident and his busted arm wouldn't postpone their safari another year, but if it did, they'd have more time to practice shooting.

On November 17, Pauline typed a letter from Ernest to Max, providing the details of the accident. Then Ernest offered an idea: "Why don't you have Scribner's insure me against accident and disease? I believe there would be big money in it. It might pay better than publishing my books. Since I have been under contract to you, I have had anthrax, cut my right eyeball, congestion of the kidney, cut index finger, forehead gashed, cheek torn open, branch ran through leg, and now this arm. However, on the other hand, during this whole period I have never been constipated."

Before the accident, Ernest had been on page 285 and confident of finishing it before Christmas. Now, he did not know when he'd have the use of his arm back, but he vowed to Max that even if he had to learn to write with his left hand or his big toe he could outwrite any writer who had hoped to see him put out of business. In the meantime, he would rely on Pauline to take dictation. He told Max, "It is fine to have Pauline here, but outside of that life is pretty dull."

For Pauline, though, it was hard to see Ernest suffering like this. She prayed his arm would heal well and soon they could return to Key West for his recovery.

NO MORE GUNS

After typing Ernest's last morphine-fueled diatribe about guns to Mike, Pauline had put her foot down: no more guns. So instead, in his next letter to Mike, Ernest rambled about the snuff racket (Mike's family had an interest in Burley's Tobacco), fishing for tuna, and a new fourteen-foot salmon rod he'd ordered.

Ernest's arm had been hurting like hell, and he complained about Max, whom Mike also had become friendly with. Even though Ernest wired Max on November 14, asking him to send *The Adventures of Ephraim Tutt* by Arthur Train and *Two Years* by Liam O'Flaherty, he hadn't received them.

Ernest said Max's office had a way of sending his mail to "any former address" he'd had instead of the current one. And he had yet to see the new edition of *In Our Time* published last month. Ernest wondered if Max was worried that he wouldn't like what Bunny Wilson had written. Ernest sarcastically complained that he might need to switch publishers if he could find one that could manage to send his mail to the correct address. He was upset about the whole business.

When Ernest finally received the copy of *In Our Time*, with the introduction by Wilson, he was not happy. Could this have been why Max delayed to send him a copy of the published book? Max had known that the only reason Ernest had wanted an introduction in the first place was for clarity—he wanted readers to understand that they were buying a previously published book, not a new creation. And Wilson was the only critic whom Ernest respected, so he had trusted him to write the introduction. Ernest had not even requested to see it before it went into print.

After receiving the copy of *In Our Time*, Ernest saw that Bunny had taken it upon himself to write a piece of criticism that included negative comments about the genesis of poetry by Ezra Pound and Dorothy Parker, both friends of Ernest's, not to mention criticizing "the romantic" ending of *A Farewell to Arms*.

Ernest had come to believe Max had double-crossed him with Bunny on the *In Our Time* introduction, that Max had erroneously thought that Ernest would be okay with someone in his own book making Ernest out as a "faking romanticist."

Maybe it was the result of the morphine, but he lay awake at night thinking about it.

A ROTTEN TIME

PAULINE ADMIRED ERNEST'S BRAVERY; she knew he was in pain and that dictating letters was a good way to occupy his time. But sometimes when Pauline was typing Ernest's letters, she would add a note of her own. On Ernest's letter to Max, she added a note to Max in pen, telling him that it was sad to see Ernest in such bad shape, in pain all the time for a month, and not sleeping at night. She encouraged Max to write Ernest letters; mail helped break up the hospital monotony.

Pauline had grown bored of typing, so when Ernest began a crazy letter to their poet friend Archie about their postponed trip to Africa, as well as other trips to Antibes and Cannes and Bordighera, she took creative liberties with the format as she typed:

> The lines
> of motors were as tightly
> packed as Fifth Avenue.
> You couldn't have thrown
> a stone in any direction
> without knocking out a . . .

She entertained herself by typing Ernest's words so they looked like poetry on the page. The letter to Archie concluded with:

> Well. Mac, I feel I've abused Pauline enough
> at pounding this mill, although she has been

trying to amuse herself by typing it very fancy,
and I hope you will show it to Mrs. M. as an

example of what a good wife can do in case you
should ever become an ex-writer like Papa.

Write to Piggott and see if you get Dotty to
write to Piggott, too. Give my best to Benchley
                              and my love to
                              Mrs. MacLeish and Mimi

When Ernest looked at the final letter, he objected to her fancy typing, so Pauline added a note asking Archie to imagine that it was just ordinary typing, and she promised not to do it again.

MONTANA
IN THE REARVIEW MIRROR

ON DECEMBER 18, 1930, Ernest sent Max a cable asking him to forward mail to Piggott. He hoped they would be leaving Montana in a few days.

Part III

1932

What Ernest Loved About Pauline

Keen editorial eye
Her family became his family: Jinny, Mother Pfeiffer
Uncle Gus's support
Strong again
Lovely figure again after Gregory's birth
"Someone to feel swell with" after a day's work
The "feeling of us against the others"
Willing to join him on adventures
Believed in the "promotion of masculine society"
Never worried like other wives
Vowed to always let him have his way
~~She could give him "little Pilar"~~
~~Her throat never got sore like his~~
~~Spontaneous lovemaking~~

RECOVERY

IT WAS HARD for Pauline to relax when she worried that she was pregnant again. The Sidley cabin was lovely, with its large living room and river rock fireplace, and space for Ernest to set up an office. But she was preoccupied with the fact that she had missed her cycle. The doctor had told her after Gregory was born on November 5, 1931, if she got pregnant again she would be putting her life in danger. She and Ernest had followed the calendar, being very careful, but perhaps their methods weren't foolproof. Ernest was worried too.

Perched on a hilltop at the L Bar T Ranch, the Sidley cabin was more spacious than the little double cabin they'd rented two years earlier with Jack, and it had a wide front porch providing a perfect vantage point for enjoying the distant peaks and river below. The Sidleys had offered their own cabin to the Hemingways out of gratitude for Pauline saving Elaine Sidley's life.

It had happened in a freak accident when the Sidleys had come to Key West for a visit. Ernest and William Sidley had been offshore fishing while Pauline and Elaine stayed on land, enjoying the Bayview Park pool. Pauline looked up to find Elaine floating facedown in the pool, quickly pulling her from the water and rushing her by ambulance to the hospital where Elaine was revived—then bringing her to the Hemingway home to recover. The Key West newspaper had even written about it: CHICAGO WOMAN DRAGGED UNCONSCIOUS FROM WATER BY MRS. ERNEST HEMINGWAY. The Sidleys insisted that from now on, whenever Ernest and Pauline came to the L Bar T, they would stay in the Sidley cabin.

The Sidley cabin where the Hemingways stayed at the Nordquist Ranch. *Courtesy Bob Richard*

In Key West, in addition to the Sidleys, Pauline and Ernest had entertained many Wyoming acquaintances while Ernest recovered from the car accident. Unable to write, or hold a fishing rod, or shoot a gun, Ernest had craved distractions. Lawrence and Olive Nordquist came for a visit, as did Chub Weaver, who took a break from wrangling on the ranch and had driven their repaired Ford from Billings and stayed to fish.

Ernest's sister Carol, Jinny, Max Perkins, Burge Saunders, and Paris friends John Herrmann, Josie Herbst, and Pat and Maud Morgan had arrived. Even Ernest's mother, Grace, showed up for a brief visit to check on her son and finally meet her grandson Patrick, who was nearly three at the time. Pauline had met Grace only once before, the day on the dock when she'd been pregnant with Patrick. She and Ernest's mother had settled into a comfortable relationship, with Pauline calling her "Mother Grace."

When Ernest could finally write again, six months after the accident, he didn't waste any time before diving into work on the bullfighting book he had titled *Death in the Afternoon*. He needed to go to Spain to gather materials for the book, and a plan had been made for Pauline and Patrick to meet him in Paris a few weeks later. Pauline had been wrapping up details on the purchase of a home they'd bought on Whitehead Street, and she also wanted to talk to Dr. Guffey about her pregnancy before leaving. She was then four months pregnant, had gained seven pounds, and planned to return from Paris to go to Kansas City again for the birth in the fall.

Little Pilar, that's what they'd planned to name their daughter. She had hoped she could give him the girl he wanted. But when their son Gregory Hancock Hemingway was born, Ernest hadn't seemed disappointed, instead proudly bragging about his size and strength.

Gregory had been delivered by caesarean like Patrick, and that's when Dr. Guffey had also delivered the grim news and the reason their current situation was so concerning. Ernest had called Guffey for advice and Pauline had taken the ergoapiol tablets the doctor prescribed to bring on her period; they'd worked in the past, but this time to no avail.

Fresh Wyoming air would be good for Pauline, with a break from her two sons, who were a handful. Thankfully they were staying with their grandparents and Aunt Jinny in Piggott. Ernest had been restless as he finished revising *Death in the Afternoon*. At least he'd be free from the distractions that he'd found in Key West: his new love of "marlin fishing in Havana" and the company of a twenty-three-year-old blonde named Jane Mason.

THE VIEW AHEAD

THE SENTRIES WERE WAITING, Pilot and Index Peaks standing guard over the valley as Ernest steered their new Ford V8 onto the L Bar T Ranch. He breathed it all in—the cool air, the scent of pine trees, the perfect tonic for his health as he continued to recover from bronchial pneumonia. He'd been in Havana in June when the marlin were running, and after fighting a strong one, he'd overheated and then got caught in a freezing squall. The sudden drop in his body's temperature was a recipe for bronchial trouble, and sure enough, it had laid him flat in bed for a week. Even now, nearly three weeks later, he still wasn't feeling like himself.

Worrying about Pauline wasn't helping his mood. Ernest had been extra careful but despite his precautions, she hadn't had her period. He told Dr. Guffey that he worried that "a certain amount of semen gets splattered around," and that his was "very virulent." They wouldn't be in this predicament if they had been allowed to practice birth control, but she wouldn't budge on her Catholic beliefs.

After Gregory's birth, Pauline had stayed in the hospital four weeks, and when she came home the doctor had insisted that she take it easy. They had been moving into their new home on Whitehead Street, with a new nurse from France who had come down with a mysterious ailment and was also in bed. Ernest had to set his own work aside and take care of their entire family plus the nurse while she recovered, just another in the series of setbacks on the book. A busted arm, traveling to Spain for photos, Gregory's birth, moving into a new home, and here he was,

149

eighteen months later, ready to get to work just as soon as Max sent the *Death in the Afternoon* proofs to Wyoming.

The book hadn't turned out to be what he'd originally hoped for—an exhaustive treatise on the sport of bullfighting. Instead it was less far-reaching. Scribner's had reduced the number of photos he could include from two hundred to seventy—but he still felt it could be sold as a classic book on bullfighting. Max read the manuscript in February and told Ernest that he thought it was a grand book, immensely important.

While he'd been in Key West this spring, waiting for Max to send him packages of proofs to edit, he'd started writing stories—they had been pouring out of him. He'd felt like he was in the best shape and he'd never written better. He'd had ten stories ready to go in a book before pneumonia had laid him flat, stories that perhaps were fueled by his new friend Jane Mason.

Ernest needed "new" to write: new experiences like marlin fishing, and new people, like Jane and her husband, Grant. On a lucky day, he'd met them on the *Ile de France* as he and Pauline sailed home from France for Gregory's birth. Jane and Grant lived in Havana, and, more luck, Grant was an executive at Pan Am, traveling the world for his job and leaving Jane home alone at their estate. Jane, with legs that went all the way to her neck, wasn't just damn beautiful; she was an accomplished sportswoman who loved hunting and fishing and was a lot of fun to be around. Pauline got seasick and didn't enjoy deep-sea fishing, plus she now had two boys at home to care for—but Jane had been available. Pauline also enjoyed Jane's company, and the two couples, Jane and Grant, Ernest and Pauline, had even double dated for a night on the town in Havana when Pauline visited.

On the drive to the ranch, Ernest had written to Jane from Scottsbluff, Nebraska, looking for someone to travel back to the States with Bumby in the fall. He knew Jane might be in London then; would she be willing to bring Bumby back with her? He closed by writing, "Take good care of yourself daughter because you are very valuable, Pauline is writing too. Much love and have a grand summer Ernest."

As he waited for the proofs in Wyoming, Ernest intended to fish and enjoy himself as much as possible. A new highway between Red Lodge and Cooke City threatened to destroy this land, his private paradise, as it brought busloads of tourists to the area and drove all the game into the safety of Yellowstone's boundaries. The construction crew had already destroyed one of his favorite fishing holes while digging for gravel and creating a dam that dried up a fork of the river above One Mile Creek.

One morning Ernest stopped at the corral to watch Ivan and Chub saddle horses for a trail ride. Both men had become his good friends. A man of many talents, Chub often accompanied Ernest and Pauline into the backcountry as their camp cook—although Pauline didn't care for him because he called her "Pauline" instead of "Mrs. Hemingway." Ivan finished saddling up Ernest's favorite horse, Old Bess, and handed the reigns to Ernest so he could ride downstream to a fishing hole.

The land surrounding the ranch was the wildest of wild, a geologist's dream, with the same magnificent rock formations found in Yellowstone— canyons, waterfalls, and jagged cliffs. One of the reasons it had remained so primitive, and without development, was because it was so rugged and remote. Now the new road would endanger that.

Ernest looked forward to Africa and the primitive country there, safe from tour buses and dude ranches. The safari had been postponed after his accident, at first rescheduled for this fall. But in the spring, when Ernest had felt the juice again, when the short stories flowed and he felt like he was working too well to leave the country, he postponed it again. Maybe next year instead of coming to Wyoming he'd go to Africa to shoot trophies.

Max had been relieved, wanting him to focus on finishing this book and starting on another one, but Ernest knew his hunting party would be disappointed. He had told Archie the news and he seemed okay with it, but he hadn't told Mike and Charles about it yet.

Since this might be his last summer at the ranch for a while, Ernest intended to enjoy it. He set out fishing with a fervor in the Clarks Fork River and high mountain lakes, sometimes with Pauline, sometimes with the guides, and sometimes alone. By the end of July he had caught one hundred fifty trout.

MOTHERHOOD

PERHAPS IT HAD BEEN CAUSED by stress or maybe the change in altitude, but Pauline's late period finally arrived, bringing a huge relief. She and Ernest would need to be even more careful than they had been in the past.

Motherhood was a merry-go-round of hiring nurses, planning travel schedules, and monitoring the children's activities—you couldn't leave them for one second without them getting into mischief. After Gregory's birth, three-year-old Patrick had tried to kill his brother in his bassinet with ant spray, and then a week later Patrick had eaten rodent poison and thrown up for two days. The house had been in total pandemonium while Pauline was supposed to be recovering in bed.

Dr. Guffey had warned her to stay off her feet for two months after Gregory's birth, but that had proved impossible—they were moving into a new home that Uncle Gus had helped them purchase. When she'd first seen it, she'd called it the haunted house because it was in such disrepair. It had needed extensive work, and when they'd returned home with their new baby, plumbers, electricians, and construction workers needed her supervision as they worked. She was the mother of an infant and a toddler; she managed a staff including a nurse, and then a construction crew, too. It was no surprise that she overexerted herself and landed back in bed at the mercy of Ernest's care.

Caring for others was not Ernest's strength, as she had learned early in their marriage when he'd left Pauline and Patrick alone in Paris, and she'd seen it again in Key West, when he'd been trying to finish the draft of *Death in the Afternoon*. With a baby's cries, a mischievous toddler demanding attention, and workmen hammering away in the background, he'd fled to a hotel room in Havana, ostensibly to chase the marlin, but Pauline wondered if he was chasing something else.

Ernest didn't allow fatherhood to alter his lifestyle at all; he still hunted and fished and traveled with his friends. And he expected Pauline to keep up. She'd seen what happened when Hadley had allowed Ernest to entertain himself: Ernest had met Pauline. Pauline didn't intend for that to happen again. Ernest had to come first.

She was trying to love motherhood, she really was, but domesticity didn't give her the same pleasure that being with her husband did. When he was away—which had been a lot lately—she missed him all the time. When he went to Spain to work on the bullfighting book, she wrote to him, "You are the punctuation and the grammar as well as the exciting story."

At least Pauline had resources to hire a new nurse, Ada, who seemed up to the task. Even Pauline's mother had complimented the way she handled Patrick, who was at an impressionable age; Mary Pfeiffer felt Patrick needed someone who understood him, because he was intelligent beyond his years and he strongly resented wrong treatment. Still, despite Ada's skill with Patrick and Gregory, Pauline's parents didn't understand all the time Ernest and Pauline spent away from the boys when they were so young and needed their parents.

Ernest had been this way with Hadley when Jack was a baby too, demanding that she leave Jack with a nurse so they could travel together alone. Shortly after first meeting Ernest and Hadley, Pauline had joined them for the bullfights in Pamplona, and she recalled Hadley had been sick with longing for her Bumby while he stayed with his nurse.

The time away from his parents hadn't affected Jack; he was a wonderful boy. On their last visit to the ranch, Jack had joined them and had fallen in love with the West, but this summer he was in France with Hadley and Paul Mowrer. Hadley and Paul had been seeing each other since shortly after Ernest's divorce—even though Paul had been married. Ironically, Hadley had found herself in a situation similar to the one Pauline had been in; however, Paul and his wife had been living separate lives for years. Their split was amicable, clearing the way for

Paul and Hadley to be together. Ernest approved of Paul, a journalist he'd known in Paris.

As she watched children playing horse tag and enjoying themselves at the ranch, Pauline thought one day, when Patrick and Gregory were older, they could come to the L Bar T Ranch too. But for now, it was her respite from domesticity, and she intended to enjoy herself.

"HEMINGWAY'S DEATH"

ON JULY 27, when the mail came with a package from Max, Ernest was ready to get to work. However, when he opened it and read the galleys, he nearly fell out of his chair.

There at the top of each proof page, he read the slug line,* "Hemingway's Death." What was Max thinking?

He'd already told him to change it last month in Key West when he'd opened a package from Max and his eyes nearly popped out of his head. Max knew he was superstitious. Ernest could have had a stroke after seeing that—was that what they wanted?

Max had apologized by saying he understood omens, but he hadn't noticed the slug line or he would have changed it. He reminded Ernest that it wasn't personal; they had just followed "the regular rule" for the slug line: the author's name, and then the first important word of the title.

And yet, when the mail truck arrived on July 27, after Max had assured him that he understood Ernest's concern—it was still there! HEMINGWAY'S DEATH.

Irritating Ernest further, Max's letter inside did not answer Ernest's question about "the words." The words, often of the four-letter variety, had caused a fight in both *The Sun Also Rises* and *A Farewell to Arms*. Scribner's had insisted that he remove certain words that might draw the

---

* A slug line is the label at the top of every page, made from the author's last name and the first word of the title of the manuscript.

157

attention of the puritanical tyranny of the Obscenity Act. They were still living in prudish times in the United States, and some writers had seen their books confiscated due to obscenity charges. Scribner's wanted to change some perfectly useful words in *Death in the Afternoon* because the censors were still alive and well, just waiting to swoop down and make problems whenever they found "the words."

Didn't people understand these words were one of Ernest's writing tools that appeared in the dialogue of real people? That was how real people talked. Once, he'd counseled his sister Carol on the effectiveness of swearing, insisting swear words were so much better than slang words; they had staying power in the language, never go out of style, and were extremely useful. People needed to understand that he used certain words because there wasn't a way to avoid them and still convey the same feeling he was trying to give the reader.

Ernest had already toned down the language for *Death in the Afternoon.* If he had included real dialogue from the bullring, the book would never get published. He never used the words gratuitously; he used them sparingly, only when no other word would do. Ernest told Max that if he couldn't print the entire word, he could at least leave the first and last letter of the word. Ernest was exhausted by the fight; he just wanted to get the damn book to the printer.

It had been a wrestling match with Scribner's since he had first sent them the manuscript. They had cut the number of photos from the two hundred he'd wanted—photos that he had traveled through Europe on his own nickel to gather—to sixteen, a ridiculous number. He'd argued that the book needed to be properly illustrated and needed more photos than that, even if he had to use his own money to pay for them. In the end, they had compromised, agreeing to include seventy photos in the book.

Last spring, he'd sent the manuscript to Dos, a writer he trusted and respected, to read. Dos thought it was a good book but told him to cut the shit—where there was too much of Ernest philosophizing—and Ernest was appreciative of his comments, taking out the material Dos objected to. Ernest hoped this book would give him the win that he needed with readers and critics. It had been three years since *A Farewell to Arms* was published, and the public was waiting for more.

Ernest quickly read the proofs and dashed off a reply to Max, asking when he would be sending the rest of the page proofs. Ernest had not yet seen a frontispiece or jacket, and why hadn't Max asked him what title would go on the frontispiece? Ernest finished his letter and put it on the mail truck to Gardiner the next day.

THE FIVE-YEAR ITCH

BLUE WYOMING SKIES without a cloud in sight stretched overhead as Pauline headed out with the guides to a fishing hole, decked out in jeans, boots, a vest, and a bandana. Despite having two children, Pauline was still the same size as when she and Ernest had first met.

Pauline and Ernest had marked their fifth anniversary on May 10. It almost went unnoticed except for a telegram she'd received from their friend Jane Mason congratulating them, and announcing that she was giving them two live pink flamingos for their Key West home as an anniversary gift.

Ernest had started getting restless after five years of marriage to Hadley—the man was always searching for new, and the "new" had been Pauline and their subsequent affair. Now five years later, could he be susceptible to the five-year itch again when he'd left for Havana on a six-day fishing trip in April . . . but stayed two months? Pauline had once been the other woman in Ernest's life; she knew the signs. She planned to keep her husband's interest, quickly getting her shape back again after Gregory's birth, and experimenting with her hairstyle, growing it into a bob and recently dying it blonde like Jane's.

While Ernest was in Havana, Pauline had made several trips to visit him under the guise of bringing things he needed, but it was really to keep an eye on him. Of course, he was charmed by Jane. What man could be immune to her charms? Drop-dead gorgeous, Jane was featured in Pond's Cold Cream advertisements; she was an international debu-tante who had come out in New York and London, and she was also a tomboy who enjoyed fishing and shooting. Most of all, she flattered Ernest and fed his ego.

Pauline liked Jane well enough, and she didn't have any real proof of an affair. Ernest had written "I love Jane" in the boat's log, but that was probably him just being playful. She chose to believe Jane was just one of Ernest's passing infatuations—she knew that his motives were sometimes those of a writer, studying people, their mannerisms, and their language that he might one day use in his writing.

She would not give him an ultimatum as Hadley had once done; she'd simply wait it out, hoping that this thing, whatever it was, would fizzle out. Maybe Ernest was simply bored. But the opposite was true for Pauline; she loved him more all the time. When she'd been in the hospital recovering from Gregory's birth she'd written, "Lovelier than anyone, and you have made me very happy, and I was never lonely with you and I love you more now than I ever did and always will."

The ranch would be good for them. Here, she had him all to herself—sharing him only with the trout and the elk. Life on the ranch was nearly perfect, but the one thing she truly missed was going to Mass; the nearest Catholic church was two hundred miles away in Powell, Wyoming. She asked Ernest if he'd drive her, and being the dear husband that he was, he agreed to take her to the First Friday service in August.

A PILGRIMAGE TO POWELL

HE'D BEEN IN A FOUL MOOD, with his chest still bothering him from the pneumonia he'd had for more than a month. Scribner's and their modifications to his book weren't helping his temperament, either. But he agreed to drive Pauline four hours to Powell so she could attend Mass; perhaps the change of scenery would do him good. Ernest was a Catholic, just not as observant as Pauline, and he didn't like to have the church in his bed—the church's stance against birth control was seriously affecting their sex life. After the latest pregnancy scare he would need to be extra careful when they made love. It was a lot of pressure on a man who loved his wife and wanted her in his bed. He could kill her if he impregnated her—yet he still wasn't allowed to use birth control.

They drove from the ranch through a changing landscape, at first through mountain country of tightly packed forests opening up to wide panoramic views. When they reached the base of Dead Indian Pass, the land outside Cody changed to sagebrush flats with red colored dirt, buttes in the distance, and plains where wild horses still ran free.

He had packed his rifles to shoot grouse along the way, and although Pauline might not have loved hunting and fishing the way he did, she was a good sport accommodating him. While he was waiting for his arm to heal, he could cast and set the hook, but someone else had to reel in the fish—and Pauline had landed a record sailfish, seven feet, one inch—the Key West newspaper ran the headline MRS. HEMINGWAY IS NEWEST HOLDER OF FISH RECORD HERE.

She was becoming a good rider and a good shot too—maybe not as good as Jane, who had won trophies, but Pauline was getting better all the time. She was even going to join Ernest and Charles Thompson to hunt bighorn sheep on the ranch this fall.

After Mass, on the rough road back to the L Bar T, they experienced a minor problem when they hit a rock and broke the oil pan, requiring them to coast into Cooke City. After four days of hunting, when they returned to the ranch on August 8, they brought back a carload of sage grouse for Olive Nordquist. Ernest thought that it had been some of the best shooting of his life.

FINAL PROOFS

THE FINAL PAGE PROOFS were waiting for him from Max. He sat down and read the whole book, starting at 6:45 AM and finishing at 4:50 PM.

They were wrapping up the last book details. Max had sent the book jacket, and Ernest thought it looked fine, but he hadn't yet received the frontispiece. He told Max the book's dedication would read "To Pauline."

Ernest was ready to get this book to the printer, as he needed the money. Max's prediction that Ernest would be able to triumph over lagging book sales caused by the Great Depression wasn't true—the Depression still held the country in its vice two years after it had begun, and it was affecting sales. Thankfully, he'd received $24,000 from the sale of *A Farewell to Arms* movie rights to Paramount, but that was the last big money he'd made. He still received royalty checks from *A Farewell to Arms*, but it had been three years since it was published, so sales were slower as readers awaited his next book.

Before he caught pneumonia in June, he had been feeling wonderful, like a kid again, writing easily. He told Max that he had three excellent stories to sell him—"Homage to Switzerland," "The Light of the World," and "The Mother of a Queen"—and he'd sell the set for $2,100, which was $9,000 less than what Ernest thought they were worth.

He signed the letter "Yours always Ernest—," and got it ready to put on the mail truck the next day.

NO WORD

ERNEST HADN'T HEARD BACK from Jane whether Bumby could travel back to the States with her, so he wrote to Jane and Grant again at the end of August. He shared details of ranch life, and told them, "Poor Old Papa has a beard you cold hunt a pack of beagles through if there were only rabbits in it. Pauline is in Grand shape, we've had the best summer ever. Haven't heard from Hadley yet about Bumby back. Have a good time and write us, love Ernest." Bumby had called Ernest "Papa" since he was a young boy, and the name had stuck.

Ernest and Hadley had managed to work out an amicable schedule sharing the boy—and when Ernest had been in Paris the previous year, Hadley had even asked Ernest's advice about Paul Mowrer possibly becoming Jack's stepfather. Paul had been a friend of Ernest's when Ernest wrote for the *Toronto Star*, and now Hadley and Paul were talking about marriage. Hadley wanted to first make sure she had Ernest's blessing, since Paul would be an influence in their son's life. Ernest wholeheartedly gave his approval.

At a young age, Jack had become an international traveler, voyaging between France and the United States to be with his mother and father. The Paris winters, however, were hard on him. The damp cold caused bronchitis, and he was susceptible the way Ernest was to sore throats and the grippe. Hadley asked if perhaps Jack could spent the next winter in balmy Key West with Ernest and Pauline, and they gladly agreed.

Ernest had hired his friend Evan Shipman to come to Key West to
work as Jack's tutor, so arrangements were falling into place—but the last
detail was to find someone to sail from France to New York City with
the boy in October. If only he would hear back from Jane.

THE MURPHYS

ERNEST HAD FIRST met Sara and Gerald Murphy in 1925 while living in Paris with Hadley. They were a cosmopolitan couple who loved embarking upon new adventures and meeting new people. Their lives were a nonstop schedule of parties and picnics, painting sets for the ballet in Paris, and hosting guests at "Villa America," their home in the south of France, where they lived *la belle vie*. They traveled with their three wonderful children, Honoria, Baoth, and Patrick; the world was their classroom. Everyone wanted to be the Murphys.

Gerald was a Yale graduate, an accomplished painter, and heir to the Mark Cross company. Tall and slender, he was an Irishman with neatly combed red hair, and somewhat of a dandy, enjoying dressing in clothes ranging from beautiful suits to dramatic capes. When Ernest took him to Pamplona, Gerald wore a pearl gray gabardine suit to the bullfights and was nicknamed "the man in the silver suit." Sara, a natural beauty, attracted the attention of men wherever she went. Ernest was one of her many fans, adoring her personality and direct manner.

The Murphys had introduced Ernest to their interesting friends, including Archie and Ada MacLeish, and Scott and Zelda Fitzgerald. Thanks to them, Ernest and Hadley had found themselves in a privileged circle of expats.

But then in 1929, the Murphys' son Patrick had been diagnosed with tuberculosis, forever changing their lives. Gerald gave up painting on the day they received the diagnosis, never touching a paintbrush again. Despite his fear of germs and hospitals, Ernest had joined Pauline, Jinny, and Dorothy Parker in Patrick's Swiss sanatorium for Christmas that year to try to cheer the poor boy with a merry party. Ernest and Pauline even named their own Patrick in honor of Patrick Murphy.

As Ernest was rounding up friends to join Pauline and him at the L Bar T, the Murphys were on the top of the list. Always game to try new things, they welcomed bringing their children to an unfamiliar land, providing them with new experiences. Honoria, fourteen, and Baoth, eleven, would bring new energy to the ranch while their younger brother Patrick remained at the family's Hook Pond cottage in East Hampton, Long Island, to fight for his strength.

Although Ernest typically didn't enjoy children until they were old enough to communicate, he had instantly liked the Murphy children upon meeting them years ago. He had once hoped for a daughter of his own, but with Gregory's birth and the doctor's instructions that Pauline could not survive another pregnancy, that was not to be. Instead, Ernest had found himself calling young women he was fond of, like Jane and Honoria, "daughter" as a term of affection.

Ernest and Lawrence Nordquist had been hunting in the high country, and when they returned to the ranch, the Murphys had arrived. The friends had a happy reunion at the ranch, and Chub and Ivan prepared the horses and provisions for a pack trip to Crazy Lakes, where they would fish and camp during the next several weeks.

HONORIA IN LOVE

EACH MORNING AT 5:00 AM, Honoria and Baoth shook off sleep and went with the cowboys to round up horses. At first Honoria worried that a weathered-looking cowboy named Hal was mean, but it turned out he was very kind, teaching her and younger brother Baoth all the words to "Red River Valley," the first song of the American West she'd ever heard.

The Murphys were assigned horses, and Honoria felt sorry for hers because his mane was so tangled. She brushed it for three days until it was "smooth as a girl's hair," then she braided it, an act that amused the hardcore cowboys. She became so horse crazy that her father joked that she might turn into a horse.

The group of six—Sara, Gerald, Honoria, Baoth, Pauline, and Ernest—set out on a pack trip to Crazy Lakes, where Ernest promised "the trout would be plentiful." Nose to butt, their horses made their way on a narrow trail through densely packed forests. Honoria worried that the horses could not fit between the small clumps of pines, but Ernest told her the sure-footed horses knew the mountains.

"Don't be afraid, daughter. You can do it," he assured her.

The riders reached camp in mid-afternoon, and the wranglers unloaded saddle bags, tended horses, pitched tents, and prepared steaks and potatoes for supper. After dinner, the group sat around the fire as Ernest wore a silly Tyrolean hat and told stories about his hunting adventures. As evening set in, Honoria became afraid.

"Will grizzlies come into our camp?"

"There aren't any around," Ernest said. "Only raccoons and rock chucks."

Honoria believed him, and she was no longer afraid.

Ernest had been in Honoria's life since she was seven, and he was one of her favorites of her parents' friends. Goofy and fun to be around, and when he spoke to her and her brothers, he gave them his full attention. The first morning at camp, as the group set out for a day of fishing, Ernest offered to take Honoria with him in a little two-person motorboat. He cut the motor when they reached an area where he thought it might be good fishing.

While Honoria trolled her line behind the boat, Ernest gently rowed.

A tug! Honoria reeled in the line with Ernest's encouragement, landing a large trout that flopped around the boat.

"Watch while I take the hook out of his mouth," Ernest said, holding the fish firmly in his hand while he removed the hook.

Honoria was not interested in the next step—cleaning a dead fish— and when he tried to show her, she waved him away, disgusted.

"Now daughter," Ernest said. "Let's grow calm while I explain to you the beauty of this creature of the water." He taught her about the scales and how to scrape them off, and that fish are clean, eating only things that live in the water.

"Can you see how the inside of its gills look like pink coral? Can you appreciate its beauty? Look at the silver shine of its underbelly and the fine feathery lines of its fins. Don't they look like lace?"

This was only the first catch of the morning—Honoria and Ernest caught many more—but it was the largest catch from their boat. When they reunited with Pauline and the Murphys, they all had caught many trout and were in a happy mood, soon helped along by the whiskey the grown-ups drank.

Chub Weaver was their camp cook, and he fried the trout over an open flame. Honoria thought they tasted unlike any fish she had ever eaten, "sweet like nectar." When Honoria and Baoth were tucked into their tent for the night, they heard Dow-Dow—their pet name for their father—singing as he strolled through the woods. When he heard them laughing, he came to their tent and serenaded them until they fell asleep.

PERFECTION

GERALD MURPHY DID NOT SHARE Honoria's love for the freshly caught trout. In a letter to his friend Archie MacLeish, he complained that "streams are overflowing with trout, some up to two pounds but the fish are adequately and not badly cooked—but somehow neutralized." The local beef proved equally disappointing. Yes, Gerald had been all over the world, and yes, he had eaten many fine meals, but he didn't feel that he had a "jaded palate." He simply felt that the ranch meals were cooked with indifference; the staff simply didn't care.

When Sara dared to complain to Ernest after being served an iceberg lettuce salad with a dollop of mayonnaise and fruit cocktail, Ernest scolded her and accused her of being snooty. Though he usually admired Sara's direct observations, he was upset that Sara had offended the cook.

Still, Gerald thought Ernest's chiding was, in a way, a sign of his affection for Sara. Ernest was never difficult with people he didn't care about. Only the few people that he had admitted into his inner circle were given his attention, "for good or bad." And Gerald felt he was not in the same class of friendship with Ernest; he felt Ernest kept him at a distance. Both Sara and Gerald had noticed a change in their old friend, who seemed more irritable and distant than the Ernest they used to know.

Ernest had shared his world with the Murphys many times. When they'd first met, he invited them to ski at Schruns, where he taught Gerald to ski. (Dos Passos was there too, hopeless because of his bad eyesight, preferring to slide down the mountain on his rear.) He took them to Pamplona, and Gerald had even joined him in the bullring, barely escaping a bull's horn by waving his raincoat. And on the ranch, Ernest had taken Gerald up to check on a dead mule that was being used for bear bait.

In Paris, Ernest had entrusted Gerald and Sara with an advance copy of *The Sun Also Rises*, which they had absolutely loved, recognizing his genius. "My dear boy . . . we love you, we believe in you in all your parts, we believe in what you're doing," Gerald had written. Sara wrote a separate note: "In the end you will probably save us all, by refusing (among other things) to accept any second rate things. Bless you and don't ever budge."

And yet here it seemed he was accepting second-rate things. Gerald was in awe of the Absaroka Mountains and felt the people who lived here "hardly noticed their vast and spectacular surroundings." There were numerous horses to choose from, but they were "most indifferent to ride because nothing has been demanded of them." Gerald's horse was a gelding with thoroughbred blood and sire to four colts on the ranch. One of the colts had been broken the previous year, and Ernest had given it to Pauline. Yet it was only a good horse, not a horse "approaching perfection." In short, nothing on the ranch approached perfection.

Ernest was wonderful with the Murphy children. Gerald appreciated how kind and patient he had been on this trip with Honoria. But it annoyed Gerald to hear Ernest call her "Daughter." That was something that belonged to Gerald—she was his daughter. Besides the nickname his children gave him, Dow-Dow, Gerald had always called himself "Papa" too, and now Gerald noticed Ernest doing the same.

Ernest left the Murphys and Pauline at the ranch while he drove to Cody to pick up Charles Thompson, his Key West friend coming out to hunt. From Cody they would drive to a private pheasant reserve before returning to the L Bar T. Gerald hoped that the pheasants they brought back were tastier than the bland fish and beef they'd been eating.

COUNTING SHEEP

IT WAS TIME for the Murphys to return to New York; they were packing for the trip home when Charles and Ernest arrived at the ranch. Although he'd enjoyed the time with them, Ernest was looking forward to his next adventure. The bighorn sheep season opened on September 15, giving Charles only one day for his sea-level blood to acclimate to the high altitude.

The hunting party of Pauline, Charles, and Ernest headed out, riding straight up the sharp spike of the mountain where Ernest had shot the old ram on his previous trip in 1930. They stalked nineteen sheep over four days; the difficult terrain gave Charles hell as he struggled with the altitude. The ledge work was the "damnedest" Ernest ever saw—you had to be a good climber to get near the sheep. At one point, he had to take off his shoes for about two miles on a rock slide, and he fell nine times. The wind raged above tree line, blowing Pauline's Stetson off her head. And while they found sheep, the animals spooked before the hunters could get close enough for a shot.

Finally, the disappointed and fatigued party headed back down. Ernest felt it was a crime Pauline hadn't gotten a sheep after what she'd been through. She would be returning to Key West soon to work on their new home and await Jack's arrival. Ernest hoped a letter from Jane would be waiting for him at the ranch finalizing the details for Jack's trip.

WOMAN'S WORK

PAULINE EXPERIENCED MANY emotions as she packed up. She'd ridden hard all summer, caught many trout, and hunted bighorn sheep in challenging conditions. And she'd had a lovely time with Ernest. But much work awaited her at their new home on Whitehead Street, which remained a fixer-upper "haunted house."

With Uncle Gus's help, they'd been transforming the rundown house into a grand home. Pauline was supervising the addition of a bathroom in the master suite, removing partitions and plastering walls, and she wanted to get it ready for Ernest's return in a month. Patrick and Gregory would continue to stay in Piggott for the meantime. She'd stop to say hello, but there was no place for a rambunctious toddler and infant in a construction site.

She would be back in Key West in time to meet Jack when he arrived from France, though Ernest still was working on the particulars of his return. Ernest said he would contact Pauline with the details after she reached Key West.

Before leaving, Pauline wrote a note to Max on one of Ernest's letters to him, saying that she and Ernest had enjoyed a superb summer and that Ernest was in "noble" condition, "galloping about on a large black horse with a big black beard." She knew Ernest was in his element out West, playing mountain man—part of the public persona he had created. She, on the other hand, was ready to return to civilization, looking forward to seeing their sons and to creating a nest where her family would all be happy together. But she lamented that she would no longer have Ernest to herself. In Key West and Havana, he had many friends awaiting his return.

REVIEWS

THE DAY AFTER PAULINE LEFT, Ernest and Charles rode thirty-five miles to a cabin at Timber Creek that Chub and Ivan had built to protect hunting parties from cold and snow. While they were hunting, a blizzard struck, and Ernest noticed how, in a snowstorm, there was a white cleanness, and in the peacefulness "it seemed like there were no enemies."*

But Ernest knew that he did have enemies, critics who had it out for him. Despite the storm, Ernest rode back to the ranch to check the reviews of *Death in the Afternoon*, which had been published on September 23. During the ride, he'd spotted a moose in an open meadow, but couldn't shoot it because he didn't have a license. He stopped along the way to shoot six sage grouse. Old Bess trembled and breathed hard through her nostrils when Ernest fired his Colt Woodsman. He brought the sage grouse to Olive at the ranch, made himself a whiskey sour, and sat down to read the reviews.

---

* Hemingway described this 1932 snowstorm years later in *For Whom the Bell Tolls*.

AND THE CRITICS SAY . . .

Meh.

DISAPPOINTMENT

THE TWO REVIEWS in the mail were both disappointing. Robert M. Coates, the *New Yorker* critic, wrote in the October 1, 1932, issue calling Ernest out for attacking other writers and for his use of "obscene" language. R. L. Duffus in the *New York Times Book Review* thought Ernest's "style was too dense" and not as good as his previous work.

What had Ernest expected? He had a love-hate relationship with critics, and he had almost dared them not to like this book. Their comments would affect sales when he needed *Death in the Afternoon* to sell well.

In addition to the reviews, he found a letter from Max, who said that although the publishing business was bad, in his opinion, *Death in the Afternoon* was selling well. The reviews were good from a publisher's standpoint, even though Max knew they included commentary that Ernest would hate.

In addition to the reviews, Ernest saw two obstacles standing in the way of this book's success: the Great Depression and Scribner's advertising budget. Published on September 23, 1932, selling for $3.50 per copy, the first printing had consisted of 10,300 copies. Sales had been encouraging, and two weeks later there had been a second printing, with 12,000 copies sold—strongest in cities like New York and Chicago.

But maybe common readers, people who lived in smaller towns across the country, didn't care about bullfighting. One reader wrote a "Letter to the Editor" in the *New York Times Book Review* that included, "I have never so much as seen the cover of one of the 2,000-odd Spanish books and pamphlets on the subject nor after reading the utter maudlin tosh distilled by Mr. Hemingway nor do I desire to do so."

Scribner's editorial staff had created advertising copy they thought would help smooth the way for Ernest's fiction fans to buy a nonfiction book about bullfighting. Ernest had thought their strategy a mistake, asking them to revise the advertising copy to more accurately reflect the book's content. He worried that, as with his past books, Scribner's ramped up advertising before publication and then dropped it, moving on to promoting their next new book.

After reading the reviews, Ernest dashed off a cable to Jane and Hadley, still trying to coordinate Bumby's transport on the *Majestic*. After Gregory's birth the previous December, Hadley had written to him and wished him the merriment of the holidays with "better eyes, more books, and no more infants." With her pending marriage to Paul, she would no longer be his responsibility, but she would always be his friend. She still signed her letters to him with his nickname for her, "Kat," short for Feather Kat.

During that last trip to Paris, when Ernest had seen Hadley, he'd realized the city had forever changed for him—it was no longer his city. With Hadley about to remarry, the Paris apartment that he and Pauline had leased now vacated, friends who had moved on, and friends who were no longer friends, he understood that it was a young man's city. He had a new home and life in Key West, and in becoming a father for the third time, it seemed to him that nothing would ever be the same.

After writing to Hadley, Ernest sent Pauline a cable with instructions on what to do about Bumby. He was trying to find out if his oldest son had sailed on the ship, and who would meet him in New York to put him on the train to Key West.

CHARLES SHOOTS A BEAR, ERNEST SHOOTS A BIGGER BEAR

BEFORE RETURNING TO THE HUNTING CAMP, Ernest encountered Huck Mees—a legendary mountain man known for making the first ascent of Pilot Peak. Ernest asked him if he'd seen the mule bait on Pilot Creek that Ernest and Gerald had set. Huck told him the mule had been eaten entirely, the larger bones piled up neatly with the skull on top. It looked as if three bears had feasted there, including one with a track eleven inches long. It had dug a foxhole beside the bait for protection while it dined.

Ernest rode with Ivan the thirty-five miles back to Timber Creek in the lingering storm. While Ernest was away, Charles had shot a large black bear and Ernest wasn't leaving until he got his own bear.

For a week, Ernest hunted in blizzard conditions to no avail. Finally, on October 11, he rode up Pilot Creek with Lawrence where additional bait had been placed. At dusk, a black bear emerged from the thicket and began devouring the horse meat. Ernest crawled to get a good shot at it. When he was seventy-five yards away he fired, but the shot hit the bear too high, and the bear bellowed and ran into the woods. Ernest trailed it into the semidarkness by the blood track.

Ernest's mother liked to tell the story that when Ernest was a boy, he'd say, "'fraid a nothing." He had faced death in a war, in the bull-fighting arena, and in a car crash. Now, in the fading light, he crept into the emerging darkness, ready to face whatever awaited him. He was just twenty feet from the injured bear when he fired a second shot that brought the bear down. The bear was the color of Ernest's beard and weighed five hundred pounds, measuring eight feet from paw to outstretched paw, much bigger than the one Charles shot.

Satisfied that he had outhunted Charles, Ernest was pleased with their tally for the season: Charles had shot a bull elk, Ernest and Charles had shot one together, and Ernest had shot one alone. Charles had also killed two fine bucks and a bear, and Ernest had "killed a hell of a big bear."

They had such an abundance of game meat that Ernest and Charles gave some to Ivan and Chub, who were both getting married that fall, to serve at their wedding receptions. They returned to the ranch and feasted on elk and venison before preparing for the long drive back to Key West.

Ernest with two trophy elk racks and a massive black bear he shot, 1932.
Ernest Hemingway Collection, John F. Kennedy Presidential Library and Museum, Boston

LETTERS BEFORE LEAVING

ERNEST NEEDED TO WRAP UP correspondence with friends before hitting the road. It was time to set things straight with Mike Strater about calling off the safari. He'd heard that Mike's feelings had been hurt that Ernest hadn't told him about the safari earlier himself—he'd had to learn about it from Archie.

Ernest wrote to Mike, apologizing and doing his best to explain why he hadn't written sooner, that since the four men weren't in one location it made it difficult to tell them all at once, so Ernest had written them one by one—no slight intended. He hoped Mike would still be able to join him with Archie and Charles when they went to Africa the following spring.

The season for fishing and hunting was over, trout had dropped into the deep pools, deer migrated to their winter range, and elk moved into the park. Ernest wrote Lawrence Nordquist a check on October 16 for $1,629 to cover his stay at the ranch, then he packed up and drove to Cody with Charles to spend the night at the Chamberlin Hotel.

The next morning, he left fourteen letters and a manuscript—all his summer correspondence—in a mailbag at the Studebaker Garage to be mailed to Max, asking him to forward the letters to their intended recipients. When they left Cody on October 17 for the trek to Key West, Ernest wasn't sure if he would return to this part of the country. An African safari was on his mind—his next big adventure—and this land was becoming too settled. Snow swirled as they drove, making visibility nearly impossible. They had to burn a candle in a can near the

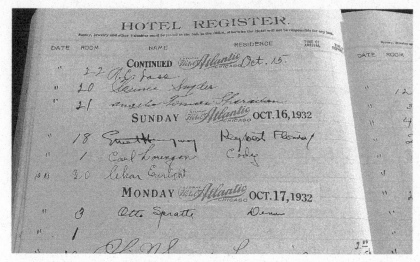

A guest register of the Chamberlin Hotel in Cody, where Ernest stayed with Charles Thompson in 1932. Renamed the Chamberlin Inn in 2005, the hotel has been renovated and remains open for business today. *Courtesy the Chamberlin Inn*

windshield to melt the ice so Ernest could see. It took them three days to outrun "un-Christly blizzards" across Wyoming and Nebraska, which Ernest described as a nightmare.

Sunny Key West would be an oasis to come home to after 2,000 miles of driving. He would write more stories and enjoy some deep-sea fishing as he considered his next project this winter. And his warm bed with Pauline awaited him.

Part IV

1936

What Ernest Loved About Pauline

Keen editorial eye
Her family became his family: Jinny, Mother Pfeiffer
Uncle Gus's support
Figure was lovely, better all the time
Strong
"Someone to feel swell with" after a day's work
The "feeling of us against the others"
Willing to join him on adventures
Believed in the "promotion of masculine society"
~~Never worried like other wives~~
~~Vowed to always let him have his way~~
~~She could give him "little Pilar"~~
~~Her throat never got sore like his~~
~~Spontaneous lovemaking~~

AFTER AFRICA

IT HAD BEEN more than two years since they'd returned from Africa, but Pauline often recalled that trip. The Serengeti had been so hot that the sun had drained the color from her nail polish in just a few hours. Driving over bumpy, dusty roads, hiking up mountains—some nights Pauline was so tired she skipped dinner and went straight to bed at camp, where she slept in huts with mosquito netting.

Pauline wasn't a fan of hunting from the car, nor did she even enjoy killing large animals that could kill her, but she'd offered to come on the safari when both Archie and Mike had bowed out, leaving just Ernest and Charles Thompson. She knew Ernest would need an audience for his trophy kills. Archie had claimed financial difficulties, and Mike said he couldn't leave work, but the real reason might have been Ernest's behavior—he'd had arguments with both men before the safari.

Africa had a unique beauty. The land's rolling plains were green from the rains, Kilimanjaro rose up in the distance, and the wildlife was magnificent—a lioness with a beautiful coat, "flocks of wildebeest," and zebras racing to cross in front of the car. Pauline wrote in her journal with a pencil, capturing their days as they traveled across the country and keeping a list of the wildlife they saw: Grant's gazelles, impalas, Thomson's gazelles (or "tommies"), giraffes, a large warthog, guinea fowl, and many other birds.

Charlie, Ernest, and Pauline had sailed from Marseilles on the *General Metinger* on November 22, 1933, traveling for seventeen days before checking in at the New Stanley Hotel in Nairobi to await the arrival of their guide, Philip Percival, who had come highly recommended by Jane Mason. It gave them time to explore the area and acclimate to the higher altitude, as they socialized with other well-heeled guests like Alfred Vanderbilt and Winston Guest, also acquaintances of Jane's.

They began the safari on December 20, 1933. One day of hunting blended into the next as Charles went out with his gun bearer and Ernest went with Mr. Percival. Some days there was friction between the men, as Ernest always wanted to shoot the biggest and best trophy and Charles was besting him. Pauline described the routine: the men went off hunting, and when they returned there were "drinks, baths more drinks [and] dinner in pajamas."

There'd been moments of tenderness, like on Christmas, when Ernest had surprised Pauline with a dustproof, waterproof watch she'd admired in Paris before departing for Africa. She'd been so touched by his thoughtfulness, and it had helped her through Christmas, missing the boys.

In the party of forty men, there were assistant hunters, gun bearers, drivers, cooks, and others. Overwhelmed by the dust, fleas, and strange noises at night, on February 3 Pauline wrote that she "felt rather dreary and men ridden." One night an animal, maybe a pack rat, bit Pauline's toe through the covers while she slept, giving her quite a start.

But her negative moods never lasted long. They visited Colonel Dick Cooper's charming tea plantation, "high and cool and swimming in flowers and vines, with a lovely view of Lake Manyara. . . ." They "played the gramophone and drank on the veranda" and slept in a big double bed.

Ernest had experienced a close call on the trip when he'd left his rifle on top of the car and it fell off and discharged—it was a miracle no one was killed. Then he had developed dysentery, suffering from diarrhea and piles, and had to be airlifted to a hospital in Arusha, where he recovered before returning to camp. When he returned, he'd lost weight, becoming very thin, but Pauline thought he'd looked extremely handsome.

With the rains coming near the safari's end, the hunting party had been pressured to leave before the roads became impassable. But Ernest had not shot a kudu, the last animal on his trophy list. Things were getting tense at camp, especially because Charles had killed a beautiful enormous kudu. They were out of time, and for Ernest, still no kudu.

On their last morning, Pauline was awakened by a racket of shouting by the hunting party, and found Ernest rejoicing. At last he'd killed a kudu. Two, in fact.

After leaving the Serengeti, they checked into the lovely Palm Beach Hotel in Malindi, where Pauline would stay for two weeks while Ernest, Charles, and Mr. Percival continued their fun with a fishing trip before heading home. It wasn't until the first week of March that they boarded the ocean liner *Gripsholm* for the long voyage to Paris before returning home to Key West.

Along the way, Lorine Thompson met them in Haifa. She brought photos of Gregory and Patrick, moving Pauline to tears. "Poor little lambs, I can see they miss Mummy," Pauline said. She had last seen Gregory on August 4, 1933, before leaving the States, and Patrick as he returned from France with Jinny on November 22.

She had known her parents wouldn't approve of leaving the boys for so long, so she'd waited until the very last minute to tell them—they thought she was only going to Paris to help outfit Ernest for the trip and would be returning home after he left on the safari. When her mother learned that Pauline was going too, Mary Pfeiffer wrote, "And so you are to journey to Africa in the near future? What part please? Just Africa is pretty indefinite. I have been looking at it on the map. Have also purchased a globe to better keep you located."

Ernest and Pauline had spent two weeks shopping in Paris before returning to the United States, arriving in New York City on April 3, 1934, where Uncle Gus hosted a reception in their honor. Ernest's reputation now included "big game hunter," publicity he approved of, as newspapers featured photos of him with his lion kill and the headline SITTING DOWN IS THE BEST WAY TO SHOOT A LION. They returned with "four lions, two leopards, three cheetahs, two rhinoceroses, and four buffaloes. Their trophy kills also included gazelles, wildebeests, impalas, klipspringers, zebras, oryxes, bushbucks, reedbucks, waterbucks, roan antelopes, topi, elands, sables—and kudus."

Despite their time away from Key West, Ernest was not ready for life as usual. Now that the safari was over, he was looking for his next new thing. He'd been thinking about buying a boat, so he and Pauline stopped at the Wheeler Shipyard in New York, where he used a $3,000 advance from *Esquire* as a deposit on a thirty-eight-foot cabin cruiser. The hull would be painted black with the name *Pilar* in white letters, the secret name Ernest had called Pauline when they were courting, and also the name for their daughter, if they'd had one.

Looking back on the safari—the scale of it, the panoramic scenes, and the time with Ernest—it was an experience Pauline would always cherish. They returned to Key West, and Ernest settled down to work on his book about their experience, *Green Hills of Africa*.

In the book, he'd written about her, "The only person I really cared about, except the children, was with me." He described her as "very desirable, cool and neat-looking in her khaki and her boots, her Stetson on the side of her head."

She'd gone with him because she knew he needed an audience; she'd wanted to make her husband happy. She got her reward when she read Ernest's manuscript: ". . . and I had no wish to share this life with anyone who was not there, only to live it, being completely happy and quite tired." She was married to the greatest writer in America, and he'd written those words about her.

When they'd returned from safari in 1934, Jane Mason had been preoccupied with her latest adventures, which included her new friend Dick Cooper, the married Wyoming oil magnate who owned the tea plantation they'd visited in Africa. If it bothered Ernest, he didn't say. He'd been consumed with his new plaything, the *Pilar*, and he'd discovered a new place, Bimini, for his entertainment. The whole family, including Jinny, nurse Ada, and the boys, had gone there in June. But after returning home to Key West, Ernest announced he wanted to go to Wyoming. He contacted Lawrence Nordquist, telling him that he was bringing Pauline and the boys to the ranch, arriving in two weeks.

Pauline was good at pivoting; just as she had put her own life on hold to accompany Ernest to Africa, she was flexible about changing plans with little notice. She went into action, packing their Western clothes, outfitting Jack and Patrick for the ranch, and making arrangements for Gregory to stay with the boys' nurse, Ada. Finally, they all piled into the car and drove out of Key West.

WYOMING AFTER ALL

CIVIL WAR HAD BROKEN OUT in Spain on July 3, 1936, and Ernest was absorbed in radio news reports as they drove to Wyoming with Pauline in the front seat and Patrick and Jack in the back. His beloved Spain, the setting for two of his novels and a number of stories, and it was being torn apart by war.

The popular front called the Loyalists, composed of republicans, trade unionists, socialists, and some leftists, had been elected by a majority. The rebel coalition, the Nationalists—made up of the officer class in the army, the police, the church, and the aristocracy—refused to accept the results. Ernest had friends on both sides and wanted to remain neutral in his public position, but he was itching to head to Spain to write about it. First, though, he had a novel to finish.

While he was in Bimini, writing short stories and waiting for a new book idea, Arnold Gingrich, his *Esquire* editor, had visited. He'd shown Arnold some of his stories, and Arnold had been very excited by what he'd read, recommending that Ernest expand one of the stories about a broke fishing boat captain into a novel. This was just the encouragement Ernest needed and he had already written thirty thousand words. He decided to go ahead and finish the book out West, where it was cool.

On August 10, they drove through the stand of quaking aspens and onto the open meadow of the Nordquist Ranch, with its sweeping view of the valley. Since his last visit, Ernest had been to bullfights in Spain, hunted lions in Africa, and discovered a new playground in Bimini, but Wyoming was always on his mind. While he was in Africa, he thought about climbing the steep terrain with Pauline and Charles to hunt sheep, and the time a gale blew Pauline's Stetson off her head. The exertion of sheep hunting in challenging conditions had helped prepare Pauline, Charles, and him for the steep terrain in Africa.

He had enjoyed time with the Murphys on the last trip to the ranch. Now poor Baoth was dead. Ernest realized they were "entering the time of life when they would start to lose people of their own age," a reminder to live life a day at a time. They had all been worried about Patrick Murphy and tuberculosis, but it was Baoth who, at fifteen years old, contracted meningitis and died. Ernest realized that the only people who really mattered to him were his wife, Jinny, and his sons.

At least Prohibition had ended. They would no longer need to import moonshine from Red Lodge and could now legally buy a drink. Despite his bitterness at the new highway, Ernest had to admit that it would make it easy to drive to a Cooke City bar.

He would follow his tried-and-true schedule of working in the morning and fishing in the afternoon and, later in the season, taking time for some grizzly hunting. But the book about the broke fishing boat captain was his focus. Writing was going well. He had worried that Max would be disappointed to learn he wasn't working on the book of short stories but on a novel instead. On the contrary, Max was delighted and thought it was much better to have the novel come out first.

CHANGING COURSE

PAULINE ENJOYED BEING back in the Sidley cabin, with its roomy layout, spacious enough to accommodate Ernest's writing and the two boys. She had become adept at moving into new environments upon Ernest's whims, whether it be returning to rugged Wyoming or experiencing his latest infatuation, Bimini.

Bimini had been lovely; they had stayed at a luxurious home owned by Mike Lerner, one of Ernest's new friends on the island. The Hemingway clan included Jack (still called Bumby at times, despite his objections), Patrick (called Mouse), Gregory (nicknamed Gigi), Jinny, and Ada. Even with Ada and Jinny's help, the boys were a lot to handle. Jack, a passionate animal lover, kept a wild bird flying freely in his room, and Patrick had set his room on fire. Pauline and Ernest had to write a large check to cover the damages. Gigi, at five, was still too small to cause much trouble.

On Cat Cay, they spent time with a young couple Ernest had met from Palm Beach, Tommy and Lorraine Shevlin, who, like Mike Lerner, were part of the "millionaire" set. Arnold Gingrich had flown in from New York to join them, and Jane Mason was there too, talking about her newest friend, "her Mr. Cooper," as she called him.

Just as Pauline had prayed for, Jane turned out to be one of Ernest's passing infatuations—albeit a long one. Pauline's strategy to look the other way instead of giving him an ultimatum had proved wise. She realized that Ernest's love of women was part of his writing, and she didn't take his flirtations seriously.

Still, she had noticed that for the past eight months, Ernest had been extremely irritable, whether from lack of female companionship or because he was between books. He picked fights with friends and acquaintances alike. In Key West, he'd heard that the poet Wallace Stevens had said some unflattering things about him, so he marched over to where Wallace was staying nearby and knocked him to the ground, breaking Wallace's hand. Another time, when Ernest couldn't open the front gate to their home, he had a fit, kicking it so hard he broke his toe. While on the *Pilar* with Katy and Dos, he shot himself in both legs when his rifle discharged and the bullet ricocheted. Katy was so disgusted by his recklessness that she stopped speaking to him. (Luckily for him, the wounds were minor.)

In Bimini, he seemed back to his normal self, happy to have an entourage. When Pauline needed to return to Key West to finish some projects on their home, she left Jinny there to keep an eye on him. She could trust Jinny to report back to her about any funny business. Pauline appreciated the deep friendship between Ernest and her sister, knowing that Jinny was one of the few people Ernest allowed to stand up to him. Ernest had returned home, leaving Jinny behind in Bimini to carry on with the fun, but he said he missed her, one of the few people he truly cared for.

Ernest and Pauline had celebrated their birthdays in Key West. On July 21 he turned thirty-seven, and the next day, Pauline turned forty-two. With Jane out of the picture, Pauline had Ernest's complete attention again. She knew he wasn't happy with her adherence to Catholic doctrine regarding birth control, but despite that challenge, she felt she had a good marriage. Ernest liked her to experiment with her hairstyles; she'd grown it out to a chin-length bob, and although she'd been wearing it blonde like Jane's, she went to an ash blonde—something he had approved of.

Now at the ranch, without a salon for miles, she'd cropped it short like a boy's again. She worked to stay in shape, holding steady at 113 pounds, playing tennis and swimming. On safari Ernest had compared her to "a little terrier"—although she preferred to be thought of as "a wolfhound, long and lean and ornamental."

While Pauline unpacked their bags in the cabin, the boys charged like wild horses down the hill, Jack to the river and Patrick to the corral.

Freedom and fresh air would be good for Patrick, as would be playing with the other children on the ranch. And Jack's big brother influence was always welcomed. He had grown into being such a lovely child, "not spoiled or self centered or silly," Pauline had told Ernest, "but a handsome, considerate, well-mannered intelligent fellow with a fine sense of humor."

BLACK ASS MOODS

ERNEST NEEDED TO PRODUCE A WINNER. Although the early numbers of *Death in the Afternoon* had been encouraging, sales had dropped off a month later, totaling just 20,780 copies—versus the 101,675 copies of *A Farewell to Arms* that had sold.

Winner Take Nothing (1933), a book of short stories, had received a mediocre reception. He had really thought *Green Hills of Africa* (1935) would put him on the map again, but to his disappointment the critics had been confused by his hybrid style. Was it nonfiction or a novel?

A few critics, including Edward Weeks from the *Atlantic*, liked *Green Hills of Africa*, finding it absorbing, and in *Time* the reviewer was touched by the way Ernest wrote candidly about his love for his wife.

But others were not as complimentary. Edmund ("Bunny") Wilson, the critic Ernest had once trusted, said the book was weak. Another critic encouraged Ernest to find more important themes than "the pursuit and dismemberment of animals and fish no matter how big."

Comments like these hurt his book sales, compounded by a too steep price tag and insufficient advertising by Scribner's. When he had returned to Key West following the release of *Green Hills*, he sunk into one of his "black ass moods," telling Sara Murphy he should blow his bloody head off. He couldn't remember feeling so low, and he had written his mother-in-law to say that the experience had made him "more tolerant of what happened to my father."

Eventually Ernest figured out that his depression was caused by not enough sleep and exercise, and the pressure he was feeling to write something that people liked. After the first of the year he had ramped up his physical activities and lost ten pounds. Lacking female distraction, Ernest searched for new inspiration and found it in the *Pilar*, which would be a key character in the new novel he was writing. Spending time on the water, on the *Pilar*, had been his salvation, and sometimes he was gone for months at a time.

The creative juice was flowing again at the ranch as he worked on the new novel about a man who carries a shipment of dynamite between Cuba and Florida and the consequences of this activity. During the first two weeks at the ranch, Ernest did little fishing, instead sitting at the desk in the Sidley cabin and producing eighteen thousand words. Unlike previous summers when the rains came and the streams were muddy, the weather this summer was ideal, with clear skies and sunshine providing a strong temptation to go fishing. He finally took three days off to hunt antelope and one more day to fish before returning and writing twenty thousand more words.

FRENEMIES

ERNEST AND SCOTT FITZGERALD, once real friends, had become friendly enemies. Ernest recognized he had behaved badly with Scott—he had even admitted it to Max—but still he let Scott get under his skin. Their relationship had deteriorated through the years as Ernest saw Scott wasting his talent due to his drinking and his crazy wife, Zelda, whom Ernest loathed.

When Scott gave *Green Hills of Africa* a lackluster review, Ernest was infuriated. Why did Ernest care what Scott said, when he considered him washed up? Earlier in the year, Ernest had been embarrassed for Scott when he read a series of articles in *Esquire* by Scott, "The Crack-Up," about his mental breakdown. What the hell was he thinking, airing his problems for the world to read?

To Max, who deeply cared about his writers, Ernest tried to keep up the pretense of caring about Scott. After all, it was thanks to Scott that Ernest had made the switch from his small publisher Boni & Liveright to Max and Scribner's. But when Scott's *Tender Is the Night* was published in 1934, a novel loosely based on the Murphys, and Scott had sent the manuscript to Ernest, anxiously awaiting his opinion, Ernest had blasted him. Rather than creating real characters, Ernest accused him of providing "faked case histories."

Not everyone felt that way. Critics had liked Scott's book, further irritating Ernest. In "The Snows of Kilimanjaro," a short story that was published in the August edition of *Scribner's Magazine*, Ernest couldn't resist getting in another dig at Scott accusing him of admiring and glamorizing the rich.

After Scott read the story, he demanded that Ernest "lay off him" in print and remove his name in any future reprints of the story. It had seemed like a strange reply to Ernest, from a man who had just totally exposed himself to the world. Didn't he know this challenge would make Ernest even more determined to write about whomever he pleased if it furthered his story?

In her book *The Autobiography of Alice B. Toklas*, Gertrude Stein had called Ernest "yellow" and a "slob." He'd paid her back in *Green Hills of Africa* without actually naming her, saying that it was a shame that she had wasted her talent by turning to malice and self-importance. Ernest was much happier without those Paris friends, no longer relevant in his life, and it wasn't his problem if people got their feelings hurt. For five years he hadn't written about anyone he knew because he felt sorry for them, but time was short and he was going to stop being a gentleman and focus on being a novelist.

It wasn't just Scott and Gertrude that Ernest had taken literary shots at; in the novel he was currently at work on, he again created characters inspired by real people. Helene Bradley—a tall, blonde beauty who took writers, painters, and big game hunters as lovers—was remarkably like Jane Mason. Other characters closely resembled Dos and Katy, Tommy and Lorraine Shevlin, and even Pauline.

THE BOYS

BEING BACK ON THE RANCH with Patrick and Jack, Pauline recalled the last visit with the Murphy children. Sara was still beside herself with grief a year after Baoth's death; does a mother ever recover from grief like that? Pauline could relate in a way with the pain she had felt about the loss of her own young brother, Max. Being thirteen years older, she had been like a second mother to him, and his death at age eleven from the Spanish flu had devastated her family.

Pauline knew that had Baoth's death had been hard on Ernest, too. He had taught Honoria and Baoth to fish, and had entertained them with songs and stories around the campfire. Even though Ernest told people that he considered parenting a part-time job, Pauline saw his patience with his sons. He'd taken Patrick with him on the *Pilar* and bragged to Pauline's mother that Patrick was a good companion, and, admitting that he might be prejudiced, but he thought Patrick was very smart. Ernest told her that Gregory was still too young to tell much about yet.

Pauline realized it appeared she preferred Patrick's company to little Gigi's, but that was because at age eight, Patrick could hold a conversation with an adult. Gigi, at five, was not able to keep up with his brother yet and was sometimes misunderstood.

Jack was often with them on school breaks since returning to the United States, after Paul Mowrer had become managing editor of the *Chicago Daily News*, making it much easier to coordinate his travel than when they had been arranging transatlantic passage from Paris. Jack was an important part of the family, and Pauline had asked Uncle Gus to make a trust for Jack like he'd done for the rest of the family.

When Jack had first visited the ranch, he could hardly contain his excitement at being a wrangler and learning to fish, and Pauline now saw the same excitement in Patrick. He didn't come down off his horse for twelve hours except to eat. Ernest had joked that Patrick would be bowlegged after this season.

Her parents didn't approve of splitting the boys up, sending Gregory off with Ada to Syracuse while Patrick visited them in Piggott, nor did they understand the amount of time Pauline and Ernest left the boys in others' care. But her parents were getting older and were from a different time. Pauline and Ernest had other friends in their circle, like the Coopers, who left their children with relatives while they traveled the world. It wasn't uncommon in well-traveled families like theirs.

With freedom from caring for Gregory—as Patrick and Jack explored the ranch on their own—Pauline could make sure to be available for rides and picnics and fishing whenever Ernest finished work. Jane might not be in the picture, but Ernest's new love, the *Pilar*, had been taking him away from Pauline for months at a time as he fished in Havana and Bimini. Finally, she had him all to herself again, smoothing the way for whatever he needed, even though sometimes he bristled at her doting on him.

In the years since they'd returned from Africa, she took comfort in what he'd written about her in *Green Hills of Africa*. But in his new short story, "The Snows of Kilimanjaro," published just this month in *Esquire*, his words were not as flattering. The protagonist's wife, Helen, shared some of Pauline's attributes, and not always in a good way. She told herself it was only fiction and that was just how Ernest wrote, basing characters on real people but then fictionalizing them. At least that's what she tried to believe.

THE RICH

ERNEST WAS STARTING to feel bitter about the wealthy people who surrounded him, like his in-laws and his new friends on Bimini. This bitterness was showing up in his writing.

In "The Snows of Kilimanjaro," Harry Walden has contracted gangrene on safari and is dying in an African camp while his wife, Helen, helplessly watches. He blames Helen and her money for making him soft.

When Ernest finished writing the story, he created a list of possible titles:

"The End of a Marriage"

"Marriage Is a Dangerous Game"

"A Marriage Has Been Terminated"

"Through Darkest Marriage"

Ernest's greatest fear in life was losing his talent—writing was what gave him pleasure in life—and as he waited to have another hit novel, he blamed others for his lack of recent success. In the seven years since *A Farewell to Arms* was published, Pauline had become even stricter in her observance of Catholic prescriptions. She was still paying for her guilt over having had an affair with him when he was a married man and going against the church, and she was motivated to be even more pious as years passed—a great inconvenience. In addition, he felt her money wasn't good for him, and he was conflicted over enjoying the wonderful things money could buy versus living without the benefits of Pauline's wealth.

In Bimini, Ernest had discovered a playground for the superrich like Mike Lerner and Tommy Shevlin and Bill Leeds, whose yacht the *Moana* was too large for the harbor. Of course, there were wealthy people in Key West, but not like the Bimini group. In Oak Park, Ernest had grown up around affluent families and had wanted to be part of them, but this was a whole new class, and he found himself conflicted. He enjoyed their company and considered them friends, but at the same time he despised their wealth, writing about them in "The Snows of Kilimanjaro."

His felt that his own relatives, the Pfeiffers, couldn't resist reminding him that he had benefited from their generosity, and it made him resentful. When Mary Pfeiffer mentioned in a letter that he had "a fairy godfather," referring to the financial help Uncle Gus had given him, or when Uncle Gus asked him to return the small refund check from the safari, these little digs reminded him who held the purse strings.

Ernest had published another story about the rich, "The Short Happy Life of Francis Macomber," in the September issue of *Cosmopolitan*. It was the story of American sportsman Francis Macomber and his wife, Margot, on safari in Africa. When confronted with a wounded lion, the husband shows his fear, and his cowardice disgusts his wife. She leaves their bed in the middle of the night to join their hunting guide Wilson in his bed—Wilson had bravely killed the lion. Some readers felt that the character of Margot Macomber, described as having a perfect oval face and wearing her hair in a knot at the nape of her neck, sounded similar to Jane Mason.

Maybe what he liked about the ranch was the simplicity of the people who lived there, straight shooters like Lawrence Nordquist and Chub Weaver, whom Pauline and Ernest had hired for seventy-five dollars a month to be their "cook, factotum, and outdoor instructor for the young" during this stay. Hard-working, down-to-earth people—so different from the Bimini jet-setters.

And yet, Ernest liked to have an audience when he played mountain man, and the rich had idle time on their hands to drop everything and come to Wyoming for sport. He found ready adventurers when he invited Tommy and Lorraine Shevlin to join Pauline and him in September to hunt antelope, elk, and grizzlies.

TOMMY BOY

In Bimini, Tommy Shevlin spotted Ernest at the Fountain of Youth bar. Tommy had read *Death in the Afternoon*, and he recognized Ernest, so he approached him. "Aren't you Mr. Hemingway?"

"Nobody calls me Mr. Hemingway here," Ernest replied.

"We've spent the summer watching bullfights in Spain and I've read your book and thought it was marvelous," Tommy said. But he had to disagree with Ernest on his opinion about one of the bullfighters in the book.

Ernest set down his drink. "How many bullfights did you see?"

"Possibly twenty."

"You can talk to me when you've seen maybe three hundred," Ernest said, and turned his back.

"I'm sorry, I didn't mean to criticize at all," Tommy said.

"Oh shut up about it and let's have drinks."

That's how their friendship had started. Later that day the two men sparred on the beach. Tommy realized Ernest was a puncher, a slugger. Ernest told Tommy, "You live under your left shoulder."

Tommy and Ernest shared a love of the sporting life, and Tommy admired Ernest's intelligence and his confidence in the field and fishing. But Ernest could be awkward socially. He wouldn't have gone to a Palm Beach society party for anything in the world, partly because he was shy, and also because he didn't care anything for those people.

Tommy recognized that Ernest had a wonderful sense of humor, but you didn't want to play practical jokes on him. He didn't like to be

213

laughed at, and he had a hair-trigger temper that you needed to watch. When Ernest invited Tommy and Lorraine to the Nordquist Ranch, Tommy accepted, looking forward to experiencing a new part of the country.

When the Shevlins arrived they found Ernest clean-shaven and trim. Tommy and Ernest rode horses into the mountains to fish at Granite Creek, where they caught six rainbow trout over sixteen inches long and four rainbows over eighteen inches. Then they moved down country to hunt antelope, and Tom admired Ernest's shooting prowess. Ernest shot two bucks; Pauline shot a nice buck too, and Tommy shot a doe.

They'd been getting along well until Ernest asked Tommy to read the manuscript of the new novel. Tommy had been flattered but had misunderstood what Ernest wanted from him. He carefully read the manuscript and wrote notes telling Ernest exactly what he thought: "I like some parts of the book, including the main character. But I dislike other parts of the book . . ."

Ernest read Shevlin's remarks, becoming very angry, and threw the manuscript out the window into the snow. Ernest hadn't really wanted his comments; he wanted his praise. He left the pages out in the snowdrift for three days. Finally, Ernest dug them out of the snow and apologized to Tommy.

"I don't write," Tom said. "And just because we're good friends, why did you ask me to criticize it?"

"Well I'll be goddamned if I know," Ernest replied. "I'll never do it again."

THE ELUSIVE GRIZZLY

THE GREATEST PREDATOR in North America, the grizzly, had eluded Ernest, and he wanted to kill one. Ernest figured that Tommy wouldn't give him much competition on the grizzly hunt—he was like a lot of rich kids who can't shoot because he never practiced. In Ernest's mind, Tommy had become a big game hunter without burning the necessary cartridges, as though Ernest would declare himself a polo player just by knowing how to ride a horse. But he was a good kid whom Ernest liked.

Jack needed to return to Chicago for the start of school, so Ernest and Pauline took him to the train in Cody while Tommy and Lorraine were sent to check on the grizzly bait Lawrence had set near Crandall Creek. Would they know what to do if they ran into a grizzly? Ernest wasn't sure, but when the Hemingways returned from Cody, Pauline, Patrick, and Ernest rode into the high mountains with Lawrence and Chub to meet the Shevlins at camp and find out.

After getting settled, late one afternoon Ernest and Lorraine hiked up the trail to the confluence of Crandall Creek to check on the bait while Tommy rode up high on a ridge as a lookout. When Lorraine and Ernest heard a crashing sound through the woods they moved low behind a rock to hide.

Ernest had expected an elk would come running out but instead saw three grizzlies. The biggest one reared up on its hind legs and looked straight at them. Ernest shot two with a 30.06 rifle, one right after the other. He regretted killing two, as they were so beautiful with their bristling silver coats, but he didn't have time to decide—he'd had to act quickly.

From left: Pauline, Patrick, Tom and Lorraine Shevlin, and Ernest with the grizzly Tom shot, 1936. *Ernest Hemingway Collection, John F. Kennedy Presidential Library and Museum, Boston*

Tommy killed a grizzly two days later, even bigger than Ernest's two. Ernest insisted that they eat some of it. When Ernest was a boy, he and his friend had killed a porcupine that was terrorizing the neighborhood, and he'd proudly brought the creature home, thinking his father would be delighted. On the contrary, his father had scolded him, telling him it was wrong to kill any animal that a person didn't eat. Was Ernest remembering his father's words as he cut some steaks from the bear and cooked them medium, then made sandwiches with the rank and stringy meat between pancakes smeared with orange marmalade? Ernest devoured the sandwich with pleasure, bear fat shining on his face.

Damn if it wasn't like the kudu and Charles in Africa all over again. When Charles had returned to camp with the massive kudu that dwarfed Ernest's meager animal, Ernest had behaved badly and made Charles feel terrible. But Charles had been a damn good hunter, and Ernest hadn't expected Tommy to provide that level of competition.

To make himself feel better, Ernest challenged Tommy to a horse race back to the ranch, betting $500 that he would win. It was snowing hard. At first, Ernest was ahead, but in the final four-mile stretch, Tommy broke away, gaining the lead. It was "slippery as a bastard on the road," and the hooves of the horse in front threw mud back into the face of the rider in the rear. When they dismounted, they looked like mud statues. Pauline actually used a trowel to get the mud off Ernest.

Tommy had won the race, but Ernest was determined to beat him at something, so he challenged him to a game of craps that night. Ernest lost $900.

All told, the Shevlins were on the ranch nearly a month, and when they finally returned to Palm Beach at the end of September, Ernest was ready for them to go. They'd had a fine time despite his worries that the good hunting country had burned out; their hunting season had been a success. They'd shot antelope, two fine elk, and three grizzlies. Now Ernest wanted to get back to work.

A CHANGE OF SEASONS

THE GRIZZLY HIDE WAS BEAUTIFUL, like silver-tipped fox but thicker and longer, the hair blowing "beautifully in the wind." Unfortunately, the hair slipped when the man who was curing it didn't do it properly and ruined the hide. Ernest, who had pictured it as a wonderful rug, was terribly disappointed, but at least he had the second hide as a prize. It turned out to be lucky that had shot two grizzlies instead of one, or he wouldn't have a hide to show for his effort.

With a successful grizzly hunt under his belt and the weather turning cold, it was time to leave the ranch. He trimmed his thick black beard with nail clippers, transforming from mountain man to Key West writer once again. Ernest packed up his novel of the struggling boat captain, 353 pages written in longhand, still with much work to do on it this winter. On October 27, Ernest wrote Lawrence a check for $1,934.73 to pay their bill at the ranch, then packed up the car for the drive, stopping in Piggott for a quick visit before returning to Key West.

Although he had concentrated on his novel, Spain remained heavy on his mind. He was interested in writing about the war's effect on common people, and he was determined to make it to Spain when he finished this book, if the war wasn't over by then. He had promised Max that before leaving for Spain, he would secure the completed manuscript in a vault to ensure it would be safe in case anything happened to Ernest.

NEW YORK

IN PIGGOTT, THEY ARRIVED to find that Jinny had left for New York to find an apartment—a disappointment to Pauline, who always looked forward to seeing her sister. She thought it odd that Jinny had left before the Hemingways arrived. Why didn't she wait to see them? Although Jinny had spent time with the family and Ernest in Bimini, Pauline had hoped to see her and catch up.

Jinny's letter awaiting Pauline didn't explain her decision to leave for New York, but she did ask if Pauline could help her move into her new apartment. Jinny had always dropped everything to help Pauline and her family—babysitting, interior decorating, being available at a moment's notice whenever they needed her—so Pauline could hardly say no. Gregory could continue to stay with Ada, while Ernest would return to Key West with Patrick. They had learned that it was easier to deal with one boy at a time while traveling. Even one could be challenging, so Ernest hired a local Piggott man, Toby Bruce, as his driver for the trip home, while Pauline prepared to go to New York.

With Jane out of the picture, she wouldn't worry about who Ernest was spending time with in Key West during her absence. She had her friends Charles and Lorine Thompson to keep an eye on him. But she knew it wasn't a woman that threatened to capture Ernest's attention now; it was the war. Ernest's talk about covering the Spanish Civil War was worrisome.

Of course, she didn't want him to go to war, and her parents were dead set against it too. He was a father and husband, and his family needed him. But she knew Ernest craved the excitement he had felt years ago in Italy, and nothing could stop him once he made up his mind to do something. She had married a writer. She knew Ernest probably better than anyone else did, and despite her objections, she knew he would base his decision on what was best for him as a writer.

HELLO, ERNEST?
THIS IS WAR CALLING . . .

As ERNEST READ NEWS in the Havana paper of the Spanish Civil War, including a daily casualty count, it was becoming harder not to choose between Franco's fascist rebels, supported by the Roman Catholic Church, and the leftist reform government composed of anarchists, communists, and socialists. One of his young writer friends in Key West referred to Ernest as a Catholic writer, "because he had friends on both sides," but Ernest had set the record straight by saying that when he wrote, he tried to write without personal bias because he had friends on both sides of the war. He would make up his mind on the war in Spain when he got there and saw it with his own eyes. However, he could never support a government intent on wiping out the Spanish working class.

Things were tense at home. Pauline was back from New York and didn't want him to go to Spain. In addition, she took issue with his comments about priests and the Roman Catholic Church—like most Catholics, she leaned toward the conservative side with the church hierarchy and supported the rebels. But when the North American Newspaper Alliance asked him to report on the war for the news service, Ernest took the job.

Ernest's in-laws were surprised he would even consider such a thing as traveling to a foreign war when he had responsibilities at home. Max had also told Ernest he wished he wouldn't go, and that he hoped nothing would get in the way of the novel's publication that spring. Ernest knew he needed to finish the novel before he left—he was nearly done with revisions to his story about the fishing boat captain. He had sent it to Arnold Gingrich at *Esquire* for his opinion, and Arnold cautioned that he felt Ernest had libeled himself; the characters Helene and Tommy Bradley were too close to the real-life Jane and Grant Mason. Ernest thought Arnold's comments, protective of Jane, were biased. He suspected that Arnold and Jane had begun a secret affair after meeting in Bimini.*

As he continued work on the book, with plans to deliver it to Max Perkins in New York after the first of the year, Ernest and Pauline stopped talking about Spain to avoid fighting.

On a December afternoon, while sitting at Sloppy Joe's Bar, a chance meeting with three tourists provided a stroke of luck for Ernest. An older woman, a golden-haired young woman wearing a black cotton sundress, and a young man—possibly the young woman's husband—entered the bar. Introductions were made, and he learned the young woman was Martha Gellhorn, a writer from St. Louis—a funny coincidence that she came from where Hadley and Pauline had both gone to school many years ago. Martha was traveling with her mother and her brother. She'd recently published a book, *The Trouble I've Seen*, to acclaim, and she'd even quoted Ernest in her book, using his phrase "Nothing ever happens to the brave" as an epigraph for her novel. As they spoke, he learned she too was interested in covering the Spanish Civil War.

---

* They did have an affair and married years later in 1955 after Jane's third marriage ended.

A WOMAN WALKS
INTO A BAR . . .

LORINE AND CHARLES THOMPSON waited with Pauline for Ernest to arrive. The Thompsons had been invited for a crawfish dinner at the Hemingway home, and after a round of drinks without Ernest, Pauline asked Charles to go to town and find him. Charles headed to Ernest's hangout, Sloppy Joe's, and returned shortly, but he was alone.

Charles reported that Ernest was talking to a beautiful blonde in a black dress. Ernest had asked him to relay a message that Ernest and his new friends would meet them after dinner at Pena's Garden of Roses.

The Thompsons had become very close to Pauline and Ernest. Lorine had helped them find their home on Whitehead Street, and she and Pauline spent much time together while their husbands hunted and fished. It wasn't the first time Ernest had been late to meet them, detained by a fan or fellow fisherman, so the group carried on with dinner without him.

Later that evening, they met up with Ernest and his new twenty-eight-year-old friend. Lorine watched as Pauline tried to make the best of the evening—Pauline had seen attractive women flirt with her husband in the past. "What she felt underneath, nobody knew," Lorine later said. After events took their course, Lorine reflected that despite the story of the "chance encounter" at the bar that Martha and Ernest told, perhaps Martha had come to Key West to make a play for Ernest.

Part V

1938–1939

What Ernest Loved About Pauline

An excellent editor, the only person he trusted with his work
~~Her family became his family: Jinny, Mother Pfeiffer~~
~~Uncle Gus's support~~
~~Figure was lovely~~
~~Strong~~
~~"Someone to feel swell with" after a day's work~~
~~The "feeling of us against the others"~~
~~Willing to join him on adventures~~
~~Believed in the "promotion of masculine society"~~
~~Never worried like other wives~~
~~Vowed to always let him have his way~~
~~She could give him "little Pilar"~~
~~Her throat never got sore like his~~
~~Spontaneous lovemaking~~

A HERO'S WELCOME

PAULINE HAD BEEN surprised to receive Ernest's cable announcing he'd be coming back home from Spain in May. She typed a response, with news of the boys, the weather, the garden, and the brick wall she was building, finishing with: ". . . life here is going on just the same as when you were here and it was unattractive to you, and it won't be any different when you get back. So if you're happy over there don't come back here to be unhappy." She added in pen, "but hope you can come back and we can both be happy."

During his stint in Spain, Ernest had returned to Key West for three brief visits—each time irritable, edgy, itching to go back—making life miserable. Jinny told Pauline rumors about the Hotel Florida in Madrid where Ernest stayed with other journalists, filmmakers, and Martha. Jinny and Ernest had had a terrible row when he had visited her in New York on his way to Spain, and she had told him she could no longer condone his womanizing and demeaning treatment of her sister. Ernest had switched from telling people she was one of the people he cared about most to saying she was spreading rumors about him and trying to ruin his marriage.

Worried about Ernest's behavior, Pauline even made a desperate attempt to check on him for herself, arranging to meet him at Christmas in Paris for what she had hoped would be a wonderful reunion. Instead she sat alone in a hotel room as he claimed to be detained by the war. "War" became one of Pauline's names for Martha. When he finally arrived at the hotel one week later, their fighting was explosive, raging for two weeks—hardly the romantic getaway Pauline had planned. They returned to the States together aboard the *Gripsholm*, and Ernest remained in Key West only a month before heading back to "war."

Pauline made a decision that life must go on when he was away; he'd been home a mere eleven weeks out of the past seventeen months. So she made an effort to develop new friendships in Key West, hosting cocktail parties at their new swimming pool, which had been financed by Uncle Gus. She went to nightclubs and out to dinner, gardened, and played tennis. On the outside it appeared she had a full, busy life. In reality, all she wanted was for her husband to be at home with her.

When Ernest's plane landed at the Key West airport at the end of May, Pauline loaded up the Ford with Patrick, Gregory, and the family driver and friend Toby Bruce, hoping to avoid a confrontation by bringing an entourage. But once again, their happy reunion was interrupted, this time when a WPA worker's jalopy collided with their car on the drive back from the airport, and Ernest and the man got into a heated argument. The police arrived and arrested the two men, hauling them into police court before sending them home.

There was a period after coming home when he seemed happy. He wrote in the mornings in his studio, and swam in the new pool during the afternoons, or fished on the *Pilar*. Pauline almost believed it, telling her parents, "Ernest seems very content to be at home. . . . I am beginning to wonder if he isn't TOO quiet." And she was right. As predictable as the arrival of monsoon season, his bad temper came. One day when he found his studio locked and the key missing, he grabbed a pistol and shot the lock off the door; Pauline sent Ada and the boys to the Thompsons, safe from the fray. Later Ernest barged into a costume party with Pauline and her friends, starting a fight with the man Pauline was dancing with, breaking furniture, and mortifying Pauline.

Friends knew Ernest could be difficult. Katy Dos Passos called him the "Monster of Mt. Kisco," and he had broken off his friendship with Dos after disagreeing on politics in Spain. In addition to Jinny and Dos, he had blown up his relationship with Archie MacLeish, too, over the financing of the film *The Spanish Earth*.

After Ernest's outrageous behavior at the costume party, Pauline could no longer keep the peace. She and Ernest began battling constantly.

She'd made it clear, without actually giving him an ultimatum, that he needed to give up Martha if he was going to live with her and the boys. She believed in her marriage and would continue to fight for it, but she couldn't stand by and watch as he openly carried on an affair. Friends knew about Martha—Ernest and Pauline's bullfighter friend Sidney Franklin, and Dos and Katy, just to name a few. Pauline realized she had made a huge strategic error by not insisting on going with Ernest to Spain when he went to cover the war.

One day in July, as the Key West heat and humidity continued to build, Ernest announced that he was taking the family to Wyoming. Pauline thought the change of scenery might do them all good and embraced the plan, making a to-do list: "pack Papa's western gear, two rifles, three shotguns, one pistol, and four different sizes of ammunition; fix the cork in the water jug"; and have the new Buick (that they purchased to replace the wrecked Ford) checked out for road.

HOME, SOMEWHAT SWEET HOME

When Ernest's contract with the North American Newspaper Alliance had ended in mid-May, Martha had continued on assignments of her own, covering stories in Czechoslovakia, England, and France for *Colliers*. He didn't want to be alone, so he had no choice but to return to Key West.

As Ernest headed back to the United States, he put up a good front, telling friends, "Am going home to see Pauline and the kids and take them wherever they want to go. . . . Have neglected my family very badly this last year and would like to make it up."[1] But he was very aware of what he was doing. In February he'd told Max that he had gotten himself into a tremendous jam.[2]

During the past year, he had walked a tightrope between two lives. When he was in Europe, he could forget he had a wife and family. He was living in the moment—it was dangerous and thrilling to be a war correspondent, when each moment could be your last—with a beautiful mistress. It was so easy to forget he was married that he had suggested marriage to Martha, while domesticity and the demands of being a father and husband awaited him back in Key West.

He hadn't known if Pauline would welcome him back, and he didn't know exactly what she knew and what Jinny might have told her. When he'd gotten into the argument with Jinny at her apartment, she'd said he was "like a porcupine which sticks anyone who gets too close" and Ernest accused her of being the one sticking in the barbs.

His ship, the *Normandie*, arrived in New York City on Memorial Day, and he stayed in town briefly before heading home, visiting his friends the Allens. They had recently seen Pauline when she had been in New York, and Ernest asked if they thought she'd take him back. They weren't very encouraging.

Pauline and the boys met him at the airport and he got settled at home, resuming his routine of writing in the morning and physical activity in the afternoon. But shortly after arriving, he started to feel irritable. After living his own life in Spain, and the freedom he'd experienced, homelife felt oppressive.

Old friends had disappointed him, starting with Jinny and her gossip, as if she'd made it her mission to ruin him. Archibald MacLeish was another friend Ernest had confronted, over financial dealings during production of *The Spanish Earth*, the movie Ernest and Martha had worked on with Joris Ivens. Ernest ended his relationship with John Dos Passos in a scathing letter because Dos continued to support Jose Robles, who had been executed for treason. Ernest accused Dos of being a fascist.

It was hot and getting hotter by the day in Key West as Ernest read galleys for his latest book, a collection of all forty-seven short stories he'd written in one volume. Ernest had also written his first play, *The Fifth Column*, inspired by his experience in Spain, and he recommended to Max that they add the play to the book of short stories.

When his novel *To Have and Have Not* was published, readers and critics had complained that it was too short. Ernest wanted to counter that criticism with a book that was long with lots of good reading, a book that gave readers their money's worth.

Wyoming had always been a good place to work, and so Ernest determined they would begin the drive shortly. Before setting out, though, he sent Max the play with the promise to send the rest of the short-story galleys either en route or once he reached the ranch.

NO HOLDING BACK

THEY PACKED UP THE BUICK V8 and began the drive on August 3 with Gregory, Patrick, Jack, and Ada. Their first stop would be Jacksonville, to drop Gregory and Ada at the train for Syracuse, where they would stay with Ada's family while the rest of the family headed west.

Shortly after departing, near Palm Beach, Gregory accidentally scratched the pupil of Ernest's bad eye—the fourth time the eye had been injured. They checked into the Hotel Washington and stayed there for two days in a darkened room while Ernest's eye healed. When they resumed the trip, Ernest wore an eyepatch and dark glasses.

They made it to Jacksonville, and Gregory, at seven years old, didn't understand why he couldn't come to Wyoming too. But for now, it worked well for Gregory to go with Ada, freeing Pauline to work with Ernest on his manuscript while the two older boys enjoyed themselves on the ranch.

Two years earlier, when they'd driven across the country with Patrick and Jack, they had listened to the radio and stories about the Spanish Civil War. War, Pauline was sick of war. She had been sitting in Havana when gunshots broke out during the revolution. And she had seen the Spanish war take her husband away.

On this trip, in the front seat of the Buick, a different kind of war raged as Ernest and Pauline quarreled. When Pauline attempted to give Ernest directions, which he mostly ignored, he blamed her if he took a wrong turn.* They fought when Ernest expressed his new disapproval of the Roman Catholic Church and how it had betrayed the Loyalists, with Pauline defending the Catholic church. In Denver, they ran out of money and Ernest had to wire Max for cash.

The real reason they fought was the uninvited guest in the car: "Miss Einhorn," as Pauline liked to call her. They had not openly discussed Ernest's relationship with her, but Pauline had made it clear before Ernest returned that he was welcome at home only if he was coming home for good. Pauline prayed that Martha, like Jane, was a thing of the past.

Rain stampeded down the valley as they finally approached the L Bar T. Despite the downpour, Pauline was confident that the boys would find plenty to entertain themselves. She would focus on typing and editing the story galleys with Ernest, hoping to work through the damage that had been done.

---

* Is this unusual behavior for a man?

WORK MATTERS MOST

THE RAIN BEAT steadily down upon the cabin roof, eliminating any temptation to go fishing when the trout would hide in holes and the fishing wouldn't improve until the stream cleared. Ernest had a singular focus; sending the short stories to Max. He'd originally hoped to send the manuscript to Max by July, but he'd been waiting to hear if it would be possible to include his play *The Fifth Column* in the book—and here it was August.

When *A Farewell to Arms* had been adapted as a play, it had flopped. But he hadn't been involved in the production at all; the producers had just bought the rights from him. He hadn't even seen the play before it closed.

This was different; it was the first time Ernest had written an actual play. He'd written it in Spain, but it had seemed cursed from the start. One producer died, the second couldn't raise the money, and it didn't look like any other producers were interested at the moment, so he was considering publishing it with the short stories. He was anxious to put it behind him.

When *To Have and Have Not* debuted in October 1937, the reviews had been unenthusiastic, and he'd felt it was partly his fault. He admitted that he'd been "snooty," and he knew the critics despised you for that. His last successful book had been *A Farewell to Arms* in 1929. Since then he'd fought with critics each time he published a book.

It frustrated him to read their snide comments about his work and then to read accolades about his friends' work. When Dos published his

U.S.A. trilogy, critics loved it, noting that parts were inspired by James Joyce's *Ulysses*. Ernest felt the root of the problem was that the reviewers were jealous of him; they all wanted to be him. Plus, he knew his political views alienated some.

It had been a while since his North American Newspaper Alliance contract had ended and he'd received a paycheck. The extra days in Palm Beach for his eye to heal added expense and also delayed his efforts to get the galleys to Max.

At the ranch, he wrestled with the order of the stories and the play in the book. Should the play come before the short stories, or after? Ernest knew the right order was important to the book, and for two weeks he wrestled with the stories' order finally deciding:

"The Fifth Column"
"Short Happy Life"
"Capitol of the World"
"Snows of Kilimanjaro"
"Old Man at the Bridge"
"Up in Michigan"
"On the Quai at Smyrna"
followed by:
the Boni & Liveright version of "In Our Time"
"Men Without Women"
"Winner Take Nothing"

Ernest and Max continued to argue over "Up in Michigan." Max was worried because authorities in Detroit had suppressed *To Have and Have Not* for objectionable material. There were still censors for obscenity; why give them reasons to suppress this book? The phrase he was concerned about was still included in the story. Couldn't they just remove it?

But Ernest didn't budge. The story needed the phrase; without it, the story was pointless.* And though cutting the story from the collection would solve the problem, Ernest was against that because it was supposed to be a collection of all the stories he'd written so far. Without "Up in Michigan," it would be all his short stories minus one.

---

* The phrase was, "Oh, it's so big and it hurts so."

Another request Max had made was to amend "The Snows of Kilimanjaro," taking out the passage about F. Scott Fitzgerald. Instead of deleting it, Ernest wanted to retain "Scott" but would take out his surname—would that satisfy Max?

Once Ernest heard back from Max on whether he agreed to the order of the play and stories, he would start work on the final piece of the book, the preface. During the first weeks on the ranch, he'd worked hard with Pauline on getting the stories ready to send—no matter how much they fought, they were able to put their differences aside to work together. He still trusted her editing skills above anyone else's.

A CAUSE FOR CONCERN?

OLIVE AND LAWRENCE NORDQUIST, their dear friends, had divorced; Lawrence was now seeing Olive's niece. The Roman Catholic Church didn't allow divorce, and it certainly wasn't something Pauline wanted— she would do whatever it took to weather the current storm. She believed that Martha, like Jane, was just a phase that would soon pass.

She'd read what Ernest had written about men and infidelity in his novel *To Have and Have Not* with interest: "But they aren't built that way. They want some one new, or some one younger, or some one that they shouldn't have, or some one that looks like someone else. Or if you're dark they want a blonde. Or if you're blonde they go for a red-head. . . . The better you treat a man and the more you show him you love him the quicker he gets tired of you." As a writer's wife, she knew not to take his words personally. Pauline tried to keep his interest, in part by staying fit and changing hairstyles: she was blonde again with a bob like Martha's.

Reading his new play, she had additional cause for concern. The play was about a secret agent, Philip Rawlings, working for the Loyalists. His cover is that of a journalist who walks like a gorilla, eats raw onions, and is plagued by insomnia and nightmares. He is in love with a beautiful American correspondent, Dorothy Bridges.

Some passages resonated, like when he wrote about the places he's been—the Crillon and the Ritz, Nairobi, the long white beaches at Lamu, Sans Souci on a Saturday night in Havana—all places he'd been with her. "But I've been to all those places," says Philip, "And I've left them all behind. And where I go now I go alone, or with others who go there for the same reason I go."

Pauline was trying to look toward the future. They had worked for two weeks on the short stories, as Pauline typed his corrections. With limited access to the outside world, he was for the moment all hers. Until the afternoon he received news from the North American Newspaper Alliance.

HITLER THREATENS

WEEKS AFTER THEIR ARRIVAL, the rain still fell in the valley, and in the high country, the peaks were dusted with snow. For the first time since he'd been coming to the L Bar T, Ernest didn't keep a fishing log recording the river conditions and fish he'd caught. The weather made it easy for him to continue to stay inside and put finishing touches on the book. On August 17, he packaged the story corrections typed by Pauline with a letter to Max, along with a handwritten dedication for the book, "To Marty and Herbert with Love," and mailed the package.*

Once he sent the preface to Max, the last piece, his work would be finished, and he would need a new project to consume him. But until then, he could hunt and fish after the weather cleared.

His plans changed abruptly, however, after he was contacted by the North American Newspaper Alliance. Adolf Hitler and his Nazi Party were continuing in their quest to reunite the German Fatherland. When the map had been redrawn after the Great War and Czechoslovakia was formed, three million Germans had found themselves living there. These Germans had begun protests and provoked violence from the Czech police. Hitler used that unrest as an excuse to place German troops along the Czech border. The North American Newspaper Alliance

---

* The dedication was to Martha Gellhorn and Herbert Matthews, the *New York Times* reporter Ernest covered the Spanish Civil War with. Ernest was making a statement to the world about his relationship with Martha. However, in the end, the dedication did not appear in the published book.

wanted Ernest to cover Hitler's actions and the possibility of another world war.

The assignment provided Ernest with the perfect exit from the ranch. Pauline had been sitting by the fire when he told her, and she had begged him not to go. Explaining that it was something he felt he had to do, he promised her he wouldn't engage in combat. Not even his love for Wyoming and the L Bar T could keep him away from Martha's pull. He had already arranged for her to meet him in Paris. He couldn't stand to be away from her for another minute.

Max wrote to him one last time before Ernest left the ranch. He felt Ernest had amended the reference to F. Scott Fitzgerald in "The Snows of Kilimanjaro" very "neatly." However, he wished Ernest could completely remove Scott's name altogether. He had asked two people to read Ernest's revision, and they agreed that Scott might still feel badly. He told Ernest they'd discuss the matter in person when Ernest delivered the preface while he was in New York.

Ernest departed for New York in late August, leaving his family behind. He and Pauline were no longer two halves of the same person. Ernest wanted to go alone. Or in the very least, if not alone, without Pauline.

TIME WITH THE BOYS

AFTER THE SHOCK of Ernest's departure settled, Pauline reluctantly accepted it. What choice did she have? He was doing important work and he must go; but his absence shouldn't stop her from enjoying her time with the boys. Ernest had arranged for Toby Bruce to come to the ranch in September to pick them up, and she would enjoy her time until then.

The rains had finally ceased, and they were free to enjoy the activities they loved—riding, fishing, and exploring. Jack had rescued a little owl with an injured wing before Ernest left, and he continued to tend to it by feeding it mice while it recovered. All the boys loved animals, and Pauline tried to accommodate their interests whenever she could. In Key West they had a menagerie, including dogs, cats, goldfish, peacocks, and flamingos, so caring for a little owl didn't faze her. Patrick was a little more needy than his independent brother, complaining of a stiff neck and that he didn't have anyone to play with. Pauline thought it would be good for him to get back in school with other children. She was proud to see him growing into such a nice boy; one morning he surprised her by going out fishing by himself and catching a trout for her breakfast.

She went out riding every day and had even gone sage grouse hunting. It was odd: after a summer of fighting, when Ernest left she felt very calm about the future of their marriage. He sent her two cables, a thirteen-page letter, a postcard, and Evelyn Waugh's new book, *Scoop*—hardly the actions of a man who might be considering leaving a marriage. She wrote him a loving letter in return, thanking him and telling she missed him very much. "But I do hope you won't stay away too long. A husband should not stay away from a loving wife too long. I won't say this again as I do not want to hurry you."

Before leaving the ranch, Pauline sent Ernest one last, hastily written letter telling him that she was feeling optimistic about their future in a "fine solid way, founded on quiet confidence that everything is going to be fixed up good." She promised to write more when they reached Piggott, and closed by saying, "My you are a lovely man, and we had a lovely time out here—hate to go." On September 6, Toby packed up the car and they departed, first stopping in Lincoln, Nebraska, to drop Jack at the train for Chicago.

———————

Ten days in Piggott with the family gave Pauline plenty of time to consider her next steps. She wasn't ready to go back to Key West—September was still hot there—instead deciding to rent an apartment in New York through Thanksgiving. She would be near Jinny and could connect with her friends like Dawn Powell, friends she had lost touch with through the years. Uncle Gus and Aunt Louise would be nearby, and she could participate in culture that she missed, like going to the ballet and theater. Jack was attending the Storm King School in Connecticut, and he could come to New York for the weekends. The more she thought about it, the more excited she became.

She sent Ernest a letter telling him of her plans and inviting him to join the family there when he returned from his assignment. She let him know that she was trusting him to be doing the things he was telling her he was doing, and that "she does not hear from strangers where her husband is and with whom."

PARIS

PARIS WITH MARTHA WAS WONDERFUL, but she often traveled on assignment, a role reversal from when Ernest had lived in Paris with Hadley and was often the one leaving her behind while he was on assignment. With Martha away, he worked on some stories, sending Arnold Gingrich "Night Before Battle" as his final piece for *Esquire*. And he'd started a new novel about the Spanish Civil War.

Pauline was living in New York in a large apartment with room for Gregory, Ada, Patrick, and Jack on weekend visits. She'd written to him sharing news about her activities in the city and about his brother Leicester, who had moved with his wife to New York and gotten a job at *Country Home* magazine.

When *The Fifth Column and the First Forty-Nine Stories* was published, Pauline couldn't find a single copy on display in the Scribner's window. She was angry when she reported to Ernest about the lackluster book promotion that he wasn't there to deal with it himself. "Perhaps my dear fellow you should be shifting from your mistress—shall we call her War—to your Master."

Critics pointed out that there were only four new stories in the book, along with a political play that was propaganda. Ernest didn't hide his Loyalist sympathies, and if the critics took issue with it, so be it. His obligation was to write the truth, and his biggest obligation was to his work. He buried himself in his new novel, returning to New York on November 24, where he would stay with Pauline and the family at the apartment until the lease ran out at the end of the month. Then Ernest and Pauline would return to Key West separately.

THE MOMENT HAD PASSED

A NEW YEAR, 1939, arrived in Key West, and Pauline could not predict what it would bring, despite her clairvoyant powers. After Ernest had returned from covering Hitler's approach, she'd realized that the moment she'd felt at the ranch, her optimism about the future of their relationship, was gone. He was sullen in the New York apartment, then came to Key West only briefly before returning to New York for the premiere of *The Spanish Earth* without her. He returned to Key West for clean clothes and then immediately left for Havana. He arrived for the sake of appearances when Uncle Gus and Aunt Louise visited, or his mother, or Jack, who was there for spring break from school. But the truth was that he'd been living at the Hotel Ambos Mundos in Cuba for months, ostensibly to work on the novel, but Pauline suspected he was consumed by something else.

She continued to write newsy letters from home to him, keeping up the pretense of a marriage: he'd left behind some things he might need—underwear, swimming trunks, and she was sending him by courier the new deck shoes he'd wanted. She also sent sample menus for a nice lunch he could make with leg of lamb and mint sauce, along with details about the boys' dentist appointments, observations on the weather, and a description of her garden.

As summer approached, and she was making plans for the boys, she ran an idea past Ernest. She had been feeling overwhelmed, she wasn't sure why, but she wrote to Ernest saying that she wanted to send the boys to camp for the summer so that they could be with other children.

It would be cheaper than her renting a home in Nantucket for all of them, and it would give her some freedom. She had found a nice camp run by Australians where the boys could fish, ride, build dams, and have fun during June and July.

Ernest, however, had not been receptive, accusing her of "dumping off the boys"—quite brash coming from a man who had very little involvement in day-to-day parenting.

HAVANA NIGHTS

ERNEST HAD LEFT for Havana after New Year's, checking into a hotel to work five or six hours a day on the novel he'd started in the fall. The more pages he wrote, the more excited he became about the work, his best since *A Farewell to Arms*. This novel could be the one that readers were waiting for.

He was still waiting to hear from Max on the latest sales figures from *The Fifth Column and the First Forty-Nine Stories*, but he knew they weren't what he'd hoped. It was hard to make money as a writer when the jealous critics were all out to get you. He needed money, and he still shared an account with Pauline, but he hated asking her to send him checks. Money was one thing it seemed they were constantly discussing. When he came back from Paris, he'd thought they had $4,000 in their account, but he discovered it was down to $400; it turned out living in New York was very expensive.

He had fifteen thousand words written on the new novel—it was bad luck to talk about it—but he was going to write until it was finished. In Cuba, he would start writing at 8:30 AM and finish at around 2:00 PM, and he planned to stay there to work, no matter what. He was feeling very fit, down to 198 pounds, healthy, and happy—he had that good feeling each day after a productive day of working on a long book. It was the same feeling he'd had when things were going well on *A Farewell to Arms*.

A distraction arrived in March when Martha came to Havana to find them a place to live. He was still married to Pauline, so he continued to receive his mail at the Hotel Ambos Mundos address for propriety's

251

sake. But Martha had found them a lovely home on a hill ten minutes from Havana.

Since being back in the States, he and Martha had spent just a few stolen encounters together, including the New York premiere of *The Spanish Earth*, to which Ernest had even invited Jack to join them. Jack couldn't believe that his father would be in the company of such a young gorgeous woman.

Ernest and Martha made plans for her to join him in Havana, and it had been his job to find a place for them to live. But he'd been too busy with his writing. He could tell "Marty" was disappointed when she arrived. Not content to share his slovenly accommodations at the hotel, she set out to find them a place of their own while he worked.

When Ernest had received Pauline's letter about sending the children to summer camp, he'd accused her of trying to get rid of them for the summer. He didn't hear from her for a while after that, until she called the hotel to tell him that she'd had a health scare, rectal bleeding that the doctors thought might be cancer. He listened sympathetically and told her although he hated to stop work on his novel that was going so well, of course he would do it for her if she needed him to. He told her he'd call her the next day to hear the results of the diagnostic tests. And he also asked her to send him some blank checks; he had run out.

As Ernest hung up the phone, a lightning bolt shot through the wires and knocked him ten feet across the room. He was left temporarily speechless, with his neck and left arm paralyzed for a short time. It scared the hell out of him.*

---

* Karma.

STRUCK BY LIGHTNING

ERNEST DIDN'T CALL the next day as he'd promised. Instead, Pauline called Ernest to tell him the good news: the cancer test results were negative. The doctor thought her condition could possibly have been stress related. Ernest had seemed relieved that everything had worked out, and that he didn't have to stop writing to join her. Most of the call was spent talking about him and how he had been struck by lightning. He seemed more concerned about himself than if she had cancer.

Their African safari guide Philip Percival was in New York, and Pauline had relayed a message that he wanted to see Ernest while he was visiting. She invited Ernest to come to New York; perhaps they could go to the Louis–Galento fight together. But Ernest hadn't wanted to take time away from writing while it was going well. Infuriated that Ernest couldn't find time in his schedule to see his former safari guide—a man who had been so marvelous to them in Africa and who had become their good friend—Pauline told Ernest in no uncertain terms that she was not happy. She followed with a letter saying their plans "would be quite simple . . . and you were say a brick layer instead of a woman layer and a writer. . . . My God Papa, but you have made things complicated with this Einhorn business. There is something rotten somewhere."

He responded with a letter of his own. He didn't appreciate her tongue-lashing; maybe the lightning should have killed him and made it easier for Pauline.

Frustrated by fighting with Ernest, feeling relieved by her clean bill of health, and finding free time on her hands after finally receiving Ernest's assent to enroll the boys at camp, Pauline decided impulsively to go on a European tour with her friends Paul and Brenda Willert. She had recently received a $10,000 inheritance after the death of her uncle Henry Pfeiffer that she could use to finance her trip. She asked Charles Thompson to stop by the Key West house and retrieve her passport since Ernest was away in Havana.

On the afternoon of July 9, she wrote to Ernest, "Relax and enjoy Miss Einhorn and here I am off your hands temporarily at best. Love Pauline."

Then on the way to the ship on July 12, she wrote in great haste, "Dearest Papa, Very excited, rather frightened and certainly wish you were going. Maybe next time you will be."

THE REAL REASON

ERNEST KNEW THE REASON why Pauline was in Europe. He'd been keeping up the pretense that he lived in a Havana hotel, but the truth was that he was living with Martha at a villa she'd found, Finca Vigia ("the lookout house"), above the working-class town of San Francisco de Paula. Pauline had finally confronted him, realizing that Martha was more than a passing affair.

He was still keeping up appearances with friends and family, telling them that Pauline was "prettier all the time." Not ready to burn the bridge with his in-laws quite yet, he wrote them that he had supported her plans to go to Europe; she needed to have some fun after the cancer scare. With war threatening to break out, it could be years before they could go back to Paris. He added that he'd been working hard so he had plenty of money to send Pauline on the trip after selling *To Have and Have Not* to the pictures. (He didn't mention that she was using her own inheritance money for the trip.)

With Pauline out of his hair, he was free to live his life with Martha, but the heat was making it harder to work in Havana. He decided to take all three boys to the ranch this summer, a guy's trip. He wrote to Hadley to make arrangements to meet Jack in August at the Nordquist Ranch with Patrick and Gregory.

Typically, Pauline scheduled their complicated travel plans, but this time Ernest would do it himself. Jack knew how to get there, through the park to Cooke City, or on the new road if it was finished. Hadley responded that she and Paul were going to be vacationing near Cody at the Crossed Sabres Ranch. Ernest felt plans falling into place. Picking up Jack in Cody and driving together to the ranch would be terrific.

He and Martha would leave from Key West, he would drop her off at her mother's home in St. Louis, and then he would drive to Wyoming. Toby Bruce could take the train to pick up the boys at Camp Te Whanga in New Preston, Connecticut, and they'd all be together for some hunting and fishing at the L Bar T: fifteen-year-old Jack, eleven-year-old Patrick, and eight-year-old Gregory—his first time at the ranch.

Ernest sent a letter to his sons at summer camp telling them that he was working on his new book, writing about a snowstorm, and he realized, why not go out West and see a snowstorm? He told the boys Toby would pick them up, and they should be very good on the train. He closed the letter sending them much love and telling them he would see them soon.

THE REUNION

Shortly after his fortieth birthday on July 21, Ernest returned to Key West, packed the boys' Western clothes, hunting gear, and fishing rods in the Buick, and began the long drive to Wyoming. After dropping off Martha in St. Louis, he continued alone, giving him plenty of time to think.

He was on page 342 of the new novel about the Spanish Civil War, and he knew it was good. War was on his mind, as it looked like another world war might soon break out in Europe. During an interview with a reporter for the Key West newspaper, he stated that if war broke out, he would go to Europe. On the home front, the battle continued to rage as he found himself still married to Pauline, though he had asked Martha to marry him and they were working together to renovate their home outside Cuba.

It was all Pauline's fault. Her Catholicism had ruined their sex life. Her fragile health had prevented him from having the daughter he wanted. And if she'd gone to Spain with him while he covered the war, maybe things would have been different—he wouldn't have looked for warmth in a lovely correspondent's bed.

Her spending habits drove him crazy. He joked to Max about her trip to Europe that he'd probably need an advance to cover her spending in Paris. Just when he thought they had money in the account, he'd find it was all gone.

He owed Hadley money for Jack's schooling, and she had been understanding. Ernest had continued to feel affection for her—she was such a good woman. When he wrote to her about Jack coming to the ranch, he told her he admired her. He reminisced about some of the good times they had shared in the Dolomites, and the Black Forest, and the forest of the Irati—heaven on earth. He signed his letter with his nickname, "Tatie."

Driving past sagebrush-covered plains and fence posts that went on and on, he finally reached Cody, stopping at Crossed Sabres Ranch to meet up with Hadley, Paul, and Jack. The staff at the lodge informed him that the Mowrers were fishing at Grebe Lake, so he drove there to see if he could find them. He was in his car, parked at the end of the fire trail, listening to the radio about Germany's invasion of Poland and imminent declarations of war, when Hadley and Paul emerged from the woods.

He had not seen Hadley for eight years, since the time they sat in her Paris apartment and she asked his opinion about marrying Paul. Seeing her now, she looked well, with her red-gold hair and her face unlined.

Once, when they were married, he had taken the train from Paris to Schruns, where she and Bumby were waiting for him at the station. He recalled the sun streaming on them and how in that moment he had wished he had died before he ever loved anyone but her. But he had been returning after spending time in Paris with Pauline, and he had fallen in love with her.

The innocent love he had experienced with Hadley had been lost. They had been in Paris, with their whole life ahead of them. Hadley hadn't deserved it. She had never caused him a lick of trouble—he blamed Pauline. It was the oldest trick in the book when a wife's best friend seduces the husband. Now he felt Pauline was getting what she deserved. After all, she'd deliberately broken up his happy home life with Hadley. He'd been seduced by Pauline's money, something that Hadley didn't have, at least not at the level of wealth the Pfeiffers had.

Over time, he'd learned it was impossible to replicate that wonderful feeling he'd had with Hadley. He was not a player, as some thought; he couldn't handle more than one woman at a time. But he had gone from one to another, unsuccessfully trying to re-create that feeling.

Ernest thought Hadley and Paul made a grand couple. The three of them had talked together by the trail for an hour, discussing Jack's school progress, and what a fine young man he had become. They were on the subject of the war when Jack came down the trail—he had stayed behind at the lake for one more cast. How happy he looked to find them there together as they awaited his arrival.

Before driving back to the lodge, Paul gave Ernest a mess of grayling from their catch that day. The Mowrers drove back to the lodge to pack for their return drive to Chicago while Ernest and Jack headed to the L Bar T.

HOPE IN A LETTER

PAULINE HAD BEEN OVERJOYED to receive a lovely birthday telegram and letter from Ernest. She wrote to thank him and to tell him how pleased she was that he would be taking the children to the ranch out West, and how happy she was to be in Paris again. She was "renewing my youth and all my memories, and learning the streets and the land marks again." Once, it had been their Paris, and being back, remembering the good times, brought her happiness. She had even run into one of their old acquaintances on the street.

She had been observing the mood of the British, Germans, and French and their attitudes toward the political arena. Still, she didn't think there was a war on the horizon, despite stories in the newspapers about German mobilization.

The next day she added more thoughts to the letter, describing the trip, and "trying to give you an idea of how exciting and sportif" the Tour de France was, with pages recounting the scenery and hills, the crowds, and the masses of wildflowers. Still not finished, she set the letter aside, only to finish it on August 7, in time to send it out on the *Normandie*. She finished by adding, "DO have a good time out there with the children. Please tell me about everything if the big ones are biting and if the river is muddy and who is shooting well and how every body is. When I was unpacking yesterday at the bottom of my bag there was a little fly fish hook. Don't know HOW it got there."

When she had discovered the little hook, she had burst into tears. How did things get to be this way? Europe had not provided the healing tonic Pauline had hoped for. On the contrary, memories of Ernest were everywhere: Paris, the Tour de France, Austria, Bavaria, too many memories of their times together.

TALKING WITH BEARS

Jack and Ernest drove around the north end of Yellowstone National Park and out the northeast entrance through Cooke City. Along the way they stopped "to talk to two bears, one a cinnamon and the other black with a white blaze on its chest." Ernest enjoyed talking to bears, and Jack thought they responded to Ernest's voice and regarded him cheerfully and alertly while he spoke.

"Hey, Bear, you're looking awful damn fat. Must've been a good summer, eh?"

Sometimes they looked embarrassed when he scolded them. "Bear, you dumb son of a bitch, aren't you ashamed of yourself begging when other bears are out making an honest living, working? Bear, you're no damn good."

Jack tried talking to them too, but they ignored him. The bears seemed to know "which of us in the car was the figure of authority, and possibly, a fellow bear."

Now that Jack was nearly sixteen, Ernest treated him like a man—as when he introduced his son to Martha at the opening of *The Spanish Earth*. Jack thought Marty was nice; he also appreciated that she could cuss with the best of them, a trait he admired in a woman.

Ernest and Jack arrived at the ranch, where Patrick and Gregory were waiting for them. They all settled into the Sidley cabin, and Jack looked forward to weeks ahead of fishing and riding with Papa and his brothers.

WAR

FOR THE FIRST TIME, Ernest had all three of his sons with him at the ranch, a platoon of male company. They developed a rhythm, fishing in the morning and then, writing by the light of a kerosene lamp, he would work on his novel until late in the night.

Work on the novel came to a temporary halt early in the morning of September 3, 1939, when Ernest heard the news on his radio and ran to the lodge, shouting "The Germans have marched into Poland! World War II has started! This could not have happened if America had helped Spain!" Ernest invited ranch guests back to the Sidley cabin to listen to the news reports on his old radio that he'd carried with him throughout his time in Spain.

News of the war was a distraction, but he knew he needed to finish the novel before war took him away again. He was enjoying having his sons with him and was in no hurry to leave. As much as he moaned about the new Beartooth Highway, he could easily drive to Cooke City, Red Lodge, and Billings—ninety miles away—where he picked up Chub Weaver and brought him back to the ranch for a visit. When they reached the L Bar T, it was late at night, and they could be heard singing cowboy songs as they drove across the meadow toward the lodge. The two men had been friends for nine years.

The society of male companionship was interrupted mid-September when Ernest received an unexpected phone call from Pauline. She had returned to the United States and decided to fly out to join him. Could he pick her up at the Billings airport?

CASUALTIES

PAULINE HAD CONTINUED to write letters to Ernest during his frequent absences in the past year like a loving wife would do, choosing to believe that she still had a marriage and that her husband was working hard in Cuba on his next novel, rather than shacking up with his young mistress. But sometimes she couldn't help herself, and the words of her frustration flowed.

"Oh Papa, darling, what _is_ the matter with you. If you are no longer the man I used to know, get the hell out, but if you are, stop being so _stupid_."

On her European tour, she spent a lot of time thinking about Ernest. It had been nearly six months since they'd been in the same place together. She decided to surprise him and the boys at the ranch, the place where they had enjoyed many wonderful times. Although her attempt at a romantic reunion in Paris had been a disaster, perhaps this surprise visit would be just what their marriage needed. Either way, it was time to have a discussion. They couldn't go on like this, staying married, while Ernest lived a completely separate life from the family. She had made her feelings clear in her letters to him and was hopeful he would choose her and his sons over Miss Einhorn.

When she reached New York, she called to ask him to meet her in Billings. However, on the plane ride to Billings, she'd become ill—raw throat, fever, aching—feeling worse by the minute. Fate conspired against Pauline's happy plans.

The drive to the ranch with Ernest was long, and she felt miserable. In addition, the weather was rainy and damp, not helpful for her condition, and they were stuck inside the cabin. At first, Ernest tried to attend to her, acting as though she was a distant relative instead of his wife. He went through the motions, trying to cook some food for her while she huddled under a blanket, drinking rye whiskey for medicinal purposes. But his rote actions made it clear that she wasn't wanted there.

Trying her best to be with her family, Pauline had struggled to get out of bed, to unpack some of her clothes. But when she found the wax buttons on her favorite Paris suit melted through the fabric, it was the last straw. All her frustrations and sadness came out as she sobbed uncontrollably while Patrick tried to comfort her.

She knew Ernest was not good at caring for sick people, but this time it was different. He was restless and complained that there was nothing for him to do after work each day. Then one September day, he announced he simply couldn't do it any longer.

It was miserable, with the boys witnessing their parents' breakup, Pauline lying sick in bed as her marriage imploded. Ernest arranged for Toby to come to Wyoming and drive Pauline and the boys back to Piggott later in September. He packed his bags, loaded the Buick, and drove across the log bridge one last time, away from the ranch, to Martha's arms.

Toby picked up Pauline and the boys at the ranch, and she had the three thousand miles back to Key West to gather her thoughts. During her years with Ernest, she had given up her own ambitions at *Vogue* and made Ernest her career—as he'd gone from an unknown writer to the great writer of his time, producing nine books and numerous articles and short stories. She'd been his typist, editor, and critic, as well as his patron, providing financial support from her family.

She could see now that she had made a mistake giving up everything for him: her career, her friends, even her relationship with her boys. She had even betrayed some of the teachings of her faith to be with him, an affair with a married man, and she continued to make amends for those actions.

Now she would need to work to rebuild those relationships. But, at least, she hoped they were reparable. She had been finding Key West dull, and conversations were so limited. Perhaps she would move to New York or San Francisco, or even Paris.

She'd had eight wonderful years with him (out of twelve). But she realized that when he made up his mind to marry someone else, there was nothing she could do to stop him. She had once been the other woman; it was ironic that she had missed the early signs that it was happening to her. She had underestimated this affair with Martha. It was like Ernest's story "The Snows of Kilimanjaro," when the hunter thought he had a little thorn scratch but it turned out to be gangrene. She had thought Martha was just a little scratch.

She still loved Ernest, and she did not want to be divorced, but he had answered her question when she had asked, "If you are not the man I think you are, then you should get the hell out." Obviously he was not the man she had thought he was.

WHEN HE CAME UP
FOR AIR

SUN VALLEY, A NEW RESORT in Idaho being developed by Averell Harriman, the chairman of the Union Pacific Railroad, was actively courting a celebrity clientele, and Ernest was on the top of their list. He picked up Martha at the Billings airport and they drove through the otherworldly Craters of the Moon—craggy black volcanic rocks and acres of scorched earth—arriving in Sun Valley and checking into their suite. Ernest, enjoying the momentum he was experiencing on his Spanish Civil War novel, hunched over the typewriter while Martha entertained herself the best she could. But six weeks later she left for Finland on an assignment from *Colliers*, leaving him alone.

When he came up for air, looking around at his empty room, it was November. Ernest realized it was time to head south and give some thought to the holidays. He thought he might spend Christmas with Pauline and the boys in Key West, thinking perhaps she'd be agreeable to that. But on the contrary, Pauline wrote to him that he wouldn't be welcome if he was planning to return to Martha after the holidays.

Ernest wrote to Hadley to find out what Jack's Christmas plans were. Maybe he could have Christmas with him? The Mowrers were staying in Chicago for Christmas, but he would be welcome to join them, Hadley said, but Ernest didn't want to impose. He wanted to have Christmas with his family in Key West.

When Toby arrived at Sun Valley to drive Ernest back to Key West, he told Ernest that this time Pauline meant business. She and the boys would not be in Florida. Instead, they were going to New York to spend Christmas with Jinny.

Despite Toby's warning, Ernest showed up at the Whitehead house in Key West and found Pauline and the boys were gone, the house deserted. The staff had been given a paid Christmas holiday. Only Jimmy the gardener remained, living in the pool house. Ernest couldn't believe she was really gone, denying him the opportunity to be with his children, leaving him to spend Christmas alone.

EPILOGUE

1940

What Ernest Loved About Marty

Her spunk
She was a damned good writer
Not afraid to swear
Spontaneous and open
"Bravest woman he'd ever met"
"Would never be a dull wife who just forms herself on [him] like
    Pauline and Hadley"
Young—not an older woman like Agnes or Pauline or Hadley
Paid her own way
Friends with Eleanor Roosevelt; took him to the White House
Could maybe produce a daughter
Beautiful
She made him "so damned happy"
~~Independent~~

SUCCESS

ERNEST'S DIVORCE FROM PAULINE had been official on Labor Day, but he had made a deal with the Miami Associate Press Bureau to hold off on the news until after his new novel *For Whom the Bell Tolls* debuted on October 21, 1940. He didn't want any possible negative publicity to interfere with the book's success. The media was fascinated with his personal life, portraying him as a womanizing cad, and that wasn't the headline he wanted people to read in the news. He wanted the story to be about his new book.

In Sun Valley with Martha he had nervously awaited to hear the world's opinion of a book he felt was one of his best. The reviews were favorable! Critics called it an important addition to American literature. Edmund Wilson wrote in the *New Republic*, "Hemingway the artist is with us again. It's like having an old friend back." At the Sun Valley lodge a private switchboard was assigned to take the Hemingway calls, and a special bell-man delivered the Hemingway mail. A movie deal starring Gary Cooper was in the works for the highest price ever paid to a book for film rights.

When the reviews came out, in many ways it was a happy time, but Ernest was still smarting over his divorce negotiations with Pauline. She had not made things easy for him, the way Hadley had done; she was demanding (egged on by Jinny) a virtual pound of flesh. She didn't need the money, but she demanded it as punishment, succeeding in squeezing $500 a month support out of him for the boys. And she would keep the house in Key West, though he retained ownership of 40 percent. But most importantly, he got his freedom.

The more Pauline had delayed the divorce, extending the proceedings, the more he'd raged. She was standing in the way of his marriage to Martha. But what did Pauline think would happen? She had stolen him from Hadley, and "those who live by the sword, die by the sword." Now she knew how Hadley felt.

He and Martha had their own pet names: she called him Rabby or Rabbit, and he called her Bongie. Ernest enjoyed Martha's independence to a degree, and it was ironic that she was also a journalist and like Pauline had worked for *Vogue* in Paris. But she'd been traveling for her work too much for his liking—she had spent a whole month in New York. For a while he wondered if she really was going to marry him, and if not, he considered delaying divorce proceedings with Pauline—maybe he could get a better deal. But at last the divorce was finalized, and he and Martha were in Sun Valley on November 4, 1940, when the Associated Press ran the story.

The path was clear for their own nuptials. Anxious to get to New York City to soak up the praise about his new book, Ernest and Martha left Sun Valley on November 20, 1940, stopping in Cheyenne, Wyoming, to get married in the Union Pacific Railroad dining room with a justice of the peace presiding over the ceremony. It was almost exactly four years since they first met at Sloppy Joe's in Key West.

New York was abuzz with talk of Ernest's new novel, a literary triumph; the accolades all he had dreamed of. He and Marty attended receptions and parties while he soaked it all up, the praise, the toasts. Unlike the disparaging comments in *The Sun Also Rises, To Have and Have Not,* "The Snows of Kilimanjaro," and "The Short Happy Life of Francis Macomber," based on the women in his life, in *For Whom the Bell Tolls,* the hero, Robert Jordan, says: "You never had it before and now you have it. What you have with Maria . . . is the most important thing that can happen to a human being."

Everything in his life had gone better with Marty, and he was so damned happy. Ernest had found the fire he had needed to write. He had found his muse at last.

In the words of his character Jake Barnes in *The Sun Also Rises,* at least it was "pretty to think so."

AUTHOR'S METHOD

MY PATH TO THIS BOOK was not a straight line; I started out writing one book and ended up writing another. I wanted to share the story of the time Ernest Hemingway spent in Wyoming near my home, but as I dug deeper in my research a voice kept chiming in, and that voice was Pauline's. As I read about her role in his life and his work from 1926 to 1940, I was hooked—by a story that began back in the United States after Paris, after the birth of Patrick, their first son, that began in Wyoming's Bighorn Mountains and ended eleven years later at a cabin in the northwest corner of Wyoming. Pauline Pfeiffer could be known as "the invisible wife" compared to Hadley Hemingway, Ernest's first wife, also known as the "Paris wife"; and Martha Gellhorn, his third spouse, the war correspondent/journalist wife—both of whom have many books written about them. Mary, Ernest's fourth and final wife, assured her place in history by writing her own book.

Since most of the people I'm writing about in *Cockeyed Happy* are deceased, I drew on their correspondence to re-create their story in their words when possible. Conversations in my book often came from letters published in *The Letters of Ernest Hemingway, Vol. 3: 1926–1929*, and *Vol. 4: 1929–1931*, Cambridge University Press; or from unpublished letters at the JFK Library, which I relied heavily upon for the period from 1931 to 1940. Unfortunately, many of Ernest's letters to Hadley and Pauline did not survive. Hadley burned many of his letters, and Pauline's stated wishes asked that Ernest's letters be burned after her death. (She died in 1951.) I included quotes from letters and other documents in this book exactly as they were written, with the writers' original spelling and grammar.

Obtaining digitized versions of Ernest Hemingway's letters was often challenging. Working remotely, I could see the dates of letters but not the content in the folders at JFK, so when I requested a batch of letters it would be hit or miss what I might find. Often they had not been transcribed, appearing in his own downward slanting script with words underlined and crossed out—challenging to decipher, but also thrilling to read in his actual handwriting.

Other sources that I depended upon include Judy Slack's *Ernest Hemingway: His 1928 Stay in the Bighorn Mountains of Wyoming*, a book compiled of news clippings, photographs, and diary entries found in The Wyoming Room, Sheridan County Fulmer Public Library. In Cody, Wyoming, Robyn Cutter provided me with a legal folder of research about Hemingway's time at the Nordquist Ranch, as well as contacts of family members who had relatives who had worked at the L Bar T.

The book that I relied upon for much of Pauline's point of view was Ruth Hawkins's *Unbelievable Happiness and Final Sorrow: The Hemingway-Pfeiffer Marriage*. Hawkins has written the most thorough work encompassing Pauline's life. Labeled as the "husband stealer," Pauline had been mostly scorned or ignored before Hawkins's book, although she was the wife with him during arguably the most productive years of his life and one of the few editors he trusted, a story that wasn't fully told until Hawkins's book.

Other books I mined for details include Carlos Baker's *Ernest Hemingway: A Life Story*; Jack Hemingway's *Misadventures of a Fly Fisherman*; Honoria Murphy Donnelly's *Sara & Gerald: Villa America and After*; Linda Patterson Miller's *Letters from the Lost Generation*; and Denis Brian's *The True Gen*. You'll find a complete list in the bibliography.

Writing a book about Ernest Hemingway is challenging in the best of times, but even more challenging when you are finishing your research during a worldwide pandemic. In a single week the libraries I was depending on closed and employees worked remotely, hours were cut, emails often went unanswered. Luckily for me the majority of my research had been done by March 2020 when the JFK Library closed, but I had to make do with the resources available to finish the book. I can't thank the JFK librarians enough for their help; it was a fabulous experience to work with them.

I am only an amateur scholar compared to the numerous biographers who have put Hemingway's life on paper, however, my time spent at Goucher College earning an MFA in creative nonfiction was invaluable in this process. Thanks to the unfailing instruction of Lee Gutkind, Lisa Knopp, Phil Gerard, and Suzannah Lessard, I learned that creative nonfiction—a term some feel is confusing—means writing a nonfiction story using such common fiction tools as scene and dialogue. You don't make things up, you don't play with timelines, you tell the real story—but in a way that reads like a novel. This book is my attempt at using this challenging genre to tell the true story of Ernest and Pauline's time in Wyoming.

Note: In a crazy coincidence, when I was conducting my research, I found a series of articles written in the 1970s by Lee Gutkind, my Goucher instructor, about Hemingway in Wyoming, something he never mentioned to me in all the years I've known him. Lee's articles and research were extremely valuable in recreating Hemingway's Wyoming days.

ACKNOWLEDGMENTS

I WANT TO THANK THE PEOPLE in my life who have accompanied me on the journey to write this book. It often became a literal journey, beginning in my hometown of Sheridan, Wyoming, and traveling to Paris, then back to the Bighorn Mountains and a remote corner near Yellowstone. Lifelong thanks to my parents, Darlene and Jerry Worden, who endured having a writer in the family, accepting my choices even if they didn't always understand them, and my daughter, Anna Skrabacz, for her tireless support and boots-on-the-ground research with me, and for writing the bibliography for this book.

More family to thank for their interest in my work and words of encouragement: Daniel Skrabacz, Carolyn and Mark Skrabacz, and my dear aunt Dorothy Green. And to Anne Parsons, my friend, researcher, advisor, and editor extraordinaire—thank you for always making my work better. To the Yayas, my girlfriends since junior high: Sandy Suzor, Cyndi Lich, Heather Vanderhoef, Rita Camp, and Julie Mason—thanks for always waiting until noon to call because you knew I was writing in the morning. You are more sisters than friends; you know all my best stories. And to friends Eliza Cross, Susan Dugan, Shari Caudron, Dan Buchan—how lucky I am to have writers as friends; your valuable input helped shape this book.

To the writers of books about Ernest Hemingway who kindly answered my questions, I appreciate your generosity: Ruth Hawkins, Valerie Hemingway, Steve Paul, Chris Warren. And to Lee Gutkind— my friend, professor and writer—who knew our paths would cross again in this way? And I wouldn't have written this book if not for my literature professor at the University of Colorado, Dr. Victoria McCabe, and my high school teacher, the late Peg Weaver, both encouraging my Hemingway interest and making a difference in my life.

People who kindly provided research, contacts, photos, and help along the way include Patricia Kennedy and Joe Ban, Brian Gaisford, Lynn Houz, and Judy Slack in the Sheridan Library's Wyoming Room; Linda Fasano for taking me to Folly Ranch; Katherine Wonson for showing me the Hemingway cabin at the Bar BC; Sharon Dynak at the Ucross Foundation; and John Sutton at Sheridan College; as well as friends Povy Kendal Atchison, always my go-to photographer; Abbie Kozik; and Amy Stark. Thank you, too, Michelle Asakawa, for your superb skills copyediting my manuscript. To Paul Balaguer and Joe Yates, thanks for allowing me to join you in your love of all things Hemingway all those years ago.

The librarians at the Ernest Hemingway Collection, John F. Kennedy Presidential Library and Museum, and Sheridan Fulmer County Wyoming Room contributed the materials that became the foundation for this book, sending digitized photos and letters—with a special thanks to Kim Ostermeyer and Debra Raver for going the extra mile in their assistance. And Robyn Cutter at Park County Archives provided a treasure trove of articles, interviews, and research.

I owe a debt of gratitude to the pros at the Dystel, Goderich & Bourret agency, Jane Dystel and Miriam Goderich, for believing in my book concept, as well as Amy Bishop and Melissa Melo; and to my editor at Chicago Review Press, Jerome Pohlen, for making this book a reality, along with the rest of the team at CRP: Benjamin Krapohl, for guiding me through the process, Jonathan Hahn, for his work on the cover, and Jen DePoorter and Hailey Peterson, for their efforts on marketing and publicity.

Gratitude to my Wiesner Media family and friends at *Mountain Living* who have checked on my progress, offering words of encouragement as I finished the book. And more to the Left Bank Writers Retreat of Paris, who share my Hemingway interest and have accompanied my many visits to Hemingway's haunts in the City of Light: Sarah Suzor,

Travis Cebula, and the writers from around the world who have joined us each June.

To John Berry, at the Hemingway Foundation, Kirk Curnutt at the Hemingway Society, and Yessenia Santos at Simon & Schuster, thank you for your assistance as I navigated the circular world of permissions and for helping me obtain the materials I needed.

CREDITS

NOTES

Part I: 1928

Keen editorial eye: Ruth Hawkins, *Unbelievable Happiness and Final Sorrow: The Hemingway-Pfeiffer Marriage* (Fayetteville, AR: University of Arkansas Press, 2012), 59.

Strong again: EH to Waldo Peirce, early September 1928, *The Letters of Ernest Hemingway, Vol. 3: 1926–1929*, eds. Rena Sanderson, Sandra Spanier, and Robert Trogdon (Cambridge: Cambridge University Press, 2015), 429.

"Someone to feel": EH to Pauline, December 2, 1926, *Letters, Vol. 3*, 170.

"feeling of us": EH to Pauline, December 3, 1926, *Letters, Vol. 3*, 173.

"promotion of masculine": Pauline to EH, March 15, 1927, Ernest Hemingway Collection, John F. Kennedy Presidential Library and Museum, Boston (hereafter cited as JFK).

Vowed to always: Hawkins, *Unbelievable*, 71.

She could give: EH to Mary Pfeiffer, July 2–3, 1928, *Letters, Vol. 3*, 402.

Her throat never: EH to Pauline, March 28, 1928, *Letters, Vol. 3*, 376.

Explorers Come West

they reminded him: EH to Waldo Peirce, August 9, 1928, *Letters, Vol. 3*, 420.

Ernest recorded mileage: EH to Peirce, August 9, 1928, 420.

corner of Nebraska: Virginia K. Moseley, "Hemingway Remembered," *Barrington Courier Review*, September 27, 1979.

go out to Idaho: EH to Evan Shipman, July 6, 1928, *Letters, Vol. 3*, 408.

enormous amount of trout: EH to Waldo Peirce, July 6, 1928, *Letters, Vol. 3*, 404–406.

"Do me a favor": Moseley, "Hemingway Remembered."

in the autoambulanzia: EH to Waldo Peirce, July 6, 1928, *Letters, Vol. 3*, 405.

He'd been nineteen: Moseley, "Hemingway Remembered."

dangerously ill: EH to Henry Strater, July 6, 1928, *Letters, Vol. 3*, 407–408.

fill up the car: Moseley, "Hemingway Remembered."

one of the first: Hawkins, *Unbelievable*, 87.

"tourist cabins": Hawkins, 92.

"bloody book": EH to Archibald MacLeish, July 15, 1928, *Letters, Vol. 3*, 411–412.

six feet tall: Hawkins, *Unbelievable*, 39.

"just as much explorers": Moseley, "Hemingway Remembered."

Shit: EH to Waldo Peirce, August 9, 1928, *Letters, Vol. 3*, 420–422.

Strength in the Afternoon

"Mother is a dragon": Pauline to EH, July 31, 1928, JFK.

"or a corpse": EH to Mary Pfeiffer, July 2, 1928, *Letters, Vol. 3*, 402.

bellow, and they can drive you: EH to Waldo Peirce, July 23, 1928, *Letters, Vol. 3*, 413–414.

hunt quail: Hawkins, *Unbelievable*, 97.

"promotion of masculine": Pauline to EH, March 15, 1927, JFK.

pressed tin ceilings: Hawkins, *Unbelievable*, 21.

"praying to Saint Joseph": Pauline to EH, November 2, 1926, JFK; Hawkins, *Unbelievable*, 30.

"ambrosial": Hawkins, *Unbelievable*, 3.

alone in the kitchen: Hawkins, 3.

"locked out": Pauline to EH, October 30, 1926, JFK.

"cockeyed happy": Pauline to EH, November 22, 1926, JFK.

"Pauline has sent": Hadley Richardson Hemingway to EH, December 12, 1927, JFK.

regaining her strength: Hawkins, *Unbelievable*, 97.

"I'm not allowed": Pauline to EH, July 29 (misdated July 8), 1928, JFK.

"With you away": Pauline to EH, July 31, 1928, JFK.

"We have a little slogan": Pauline to EH, July 31, 1928, JFK.

meant to be together: Bernice Kert, *The Hemingway Women* (New York: W. W. Norton, 1983), 203.

Fifteen Girls

"shot all to hell": EH to Pauline, December 3, 1926, *Letters, Vol. 3*, 173.

"I think perhaps": EH to Hadley Richardson Hemingway, November 18, 1926, *Letters: Vol. 3*, 153.

"Give Pauline my love": Hadley Richardson Hemingway to EH, July 12, 1928, JFK.

"pure folly": Judy Slack, *Ernest Hemingway: His Stay in the Bighorn Mountains of Wyoming* (Sheridan, WY: The Wyoming Room, Sheridan County Fulmer Public Library, 2011), 149.

"all very attractive": Gaylord Donnelley letter, October 1990, in Slack, *Bighorn Mountains of Wyoming*, no page number.

"both the matador": Moseley, "Hemingway Remembered."

"Horney, that's the place": Moseley.

social event: *Sheridan Journal*, August 3, 1928.

guests had to step back: *Sheridan Journal*.

Wyoming Wine

cold beer: I constructed this scene by compiling details from Lee Alan Gutkind, "Sheridan Couple Put in Story," *Billings Gazette*, October 18, 1970; EH to Evan Shipman, August 10, 1928, *Letters, Vol. 3*, 424; and Ernest Hemingway, "Wine of Wyoming," *The Short Stories of Ernest Hemingway*, the Modern Library Edition (New York: Random House, 1938), 548.

under the table: Hemingway, "Wine of Wyoming," 548.

didn't have any beer: Hemingway, 548.

drunk at Brasserie Lipp: EH to Evan Shipman, August 10, 1928, *Letters, Vol. 3*, 424.

arrested twice: Slack, *Bighorn Mountains of Wyoming*, 138.

"light and tasting of grapes": Gutkind, "Sheridan Couple Put in Story."

"never had problems": A. E. Hotchner, *Papa Hemingway* (New York: Random House, 1966), 51.

They Got It Wrong

"Among Miss Donnelley's guests": *Sheridan Journal*, August 3, 1928.

believe everything: EH to Clarence and Grace Hemingway, February 5, 1927, *Letters, Vol. 3*, 200.

"wrote a book" and *"Seldom has a book"*: Percy Hutchinson, "Mr. Hemingway Shows Himself Master Craftsman in the Short Story," *New York Times*, October 16, 1927.

"filthiest books": Grace to EH, December 4, 1926, *Letters, Vol. 3*, 201n2.

wonderful ability: Clarence to EH, December 13, 1926, *Letters, Vol. 3*, 201n2.

"master in a new manner": Hutchinson, "Mr. Hemingway Shows Himself."

"eased off" advertising: Maxwell Perkins to EH, April 19, 1928, *Letters, Vol. 3*, 383n7.

"*getting rich*": EH to Maxwell Perkins, May 31, 1928, *Letters, Vol. 3*, 387.
"*war was the best*": Carlos Baker, *Ernest Hemingway: A Life Story* (New York: Charles Scribner's Sons, 1969), 161.

A Clean, Well-Lighted Ranch

"*someone to feel swell*": EH to Pauline Pfeiffer, December 2, 1926, *Letters Vol. 3*, 170–171.
"*like fog*": EH to Pfeiffer, December 2, 1926, 170–171.
"*Started*" meant Hadley: Hawkins, *Unbelievable*, 56.
"*cockeyed happy*": EH to Pauline Pfeiffer, December 2, 1926, *Letters, Vol. 3*, 170–171.
"*Last fall*": EH to Pauline Pfeiffer, November 12, 1926, *Letters, Vol. 3*, 140.
"*I love you so*": EH to Pauline Pfeiffer, December 3, 1926, *Letters, Vol. 3*, 173.

Wedding Pants

"*wedding pants*": Hawkins, *Unbelievable*, 98.
"*If you will*": Pauline to EH, March 23, 1927, JFK.
"*a duffel bag with feet*": Hawkins, *Unbelievable*, 98.

Taxi Service

"*With a swell cook*": Moseley, "Hemingway Remembered."
"*to grubstake him*": Moseley.
cast him as the heavy: Moseley.
"*because he was smarter*": Moseley.

A Visit to Oak Park

"*a love pirate*": EH to Clarence, September 9–14, 1927, *Letters, Vol. 3*, 286n3.

Maximum Insurance

"*It cost me*": Pauline to EH, August 9, 1928, JFK.
he drank nearly a gallon: EH to Maxwell Perkins, August 12, 1928, *Letters, Vol. 3*, 426.
"*sheepherder's madness*": EH to Isabelle Godolphin, August 12, 1928, *Letters, Vol. 3*, 425.
Always concerned: EH to Maxwell Perkins, August 12, 1928, *Letters, Vol. 3*, 426.

Angel Child

"Hurry up": Pauline to EH, July 31, 1928, JFK.
"He didn't make a noise": Pauline to EH, August 16, 1928, JFK.
Jinny had stopped: Hawkins, *Unbelievable*, 98.

Fatherhood

"shits": EH to Waldo Peirce, July 23, 1928, *Letters, Vol. 3*, 413.

Improvising

"not much worse": Gaylord Donnelley letter, in Slack, *Bighorn Mountains of Wyoming*, no page number.

Waiting for Pauline

"Mrs. Ernie": *Folly newsletter*, Sunday, August 19, 1928.

Fresh Mountain Air

ruled the household: Hawkins, *Unbelievable*, 101.
"handsome eyes": Hawkins, 101.
Dutch product: Hawkins, 101.
liked to push Patrick: Hawkins, 101.
based on Lady Duff Twysden: Hawkins, 99.

The End

Ernest would put: EH to Maxwell Perkins, April 21, 1928, *Letters, Vol. 3*, 382.

Seeing D'America

"writer of prominence": *Sheridan Journal*, August 24, 1928.
"sweet old guy": EH to Waldo Peirce, early September, 1928, *Letters, Vol. 3*, 429.
"furious foe": Maxwell Perkins to EH, June 18, 1928, *Letters Vol. 3*, 394n2.
"three big ones": EH to Waldo Peirce, September 23, 1928, *Letters, Vol. 3*, 440.

A Lady in the Car

"Now, now": Moseley, "Hemingway Remembered."

A Farewell to Wyoming

"knocking on wood": EH to Maxwell Perkins, September 28, 1928, *Letters, Vol. 3*, 457.

Part II: 1930

other wives: EH to Waldo Peirce, June 2, 1930, *The Letters of Ernest Hemingway, Vol. 4*, eds. Miriam Mandel and Sandra Spanier (Cambridge: Cambridge University Press, 2018), 304.

The L Bar T

"Have been drinking": EH to Waldo Peirce, June 2, 1930, *Letters, Vol. 4*, 303.

Uncle Gus told Ernest: GA Pfeiffer to EH, June 3, 1930, JFK.

"fishing is simply": Bill Horne to EH, March 2, 1930, *Letters, Vol. 4*, 238n1.

famous for wildlife: "North Absaroka Wilderness," Shoshone National Forest (website), United States Department of Agriculture Forest Service, accessed March 16, 2021, https://www.fs.usda.gov/recarea/shoshone/recarea /?recid=80897.

"I'm a writer": Lee Alan Gutkind, "Fishing, Writing, Drinking," *Billings Gazette*, October 25, 1970.

Jack's Room

bank president's step-grandson: Jack Hemingway, *Misadventures of a Fly Fisherman* (Dallas: Taylor Publishing, 1986), 13.

Pauline's Respite

"hobo" and "I don't know": Hawkins, *Unbelievable*, 121.

The World Changed

heaven would be: EH to F. Scott Fitzgerald, July 1, 1925, *Letters, Vol. 2*, 358–359.

"Taty, I felt so sorry": Kert, *Hemingway Women*, 215.

"I have finished": James Aswell, "Sunday Supplement," *Richmond Times Dispatch*, October 6, 1929.

"Hemingway's A Farewell to Arms": John Dos Passos, *New Masses*, December 1, 1929.

"belly up": EH to Waldo Peirce, June 2, 1930, *Letters, Vol. 4*, 303–304.

retail and wholesale: EH to Allan Tate, June 3, 1930, *Letters, Vol. 4*, 310.

Then There Were the Distractions

"couldn't learn anything": Gutkind, "Fishing, Writing, Drinking."
"fishing is going to be": Gutkind.

Flaying Dead Horses

"stop and flay": EH to Maxwell Perkins, July 24, 1930, *Letters, Vol. 4*, 334.
"a bear with carbuncles": EH to Clarence and Grace Hall Hemingway, July 15, 1928, *Letters, Vol. 3*, 409–410.
"I want it to be the book": EH to Maxwell Perkins, July 24, 1930, *Letters, Vol. 4*, 334–336.
"This is a good place": EH to Perkins, July 24, 1930, 334–336.

Letters from Piggott

Pauline received a letter: Mary Pfeiffer to Pauline and EH, July 30, 1930, Princeton University Library Special Collections, Princeton, NJ (hereafter cited as PUL).
"Get a good strong anchor": Pfeiffer to Pauline and EH, July 30, 1930, PUL.
would become delirious: Hawkins, *Unbelievable*, 111.
Her mother had recommended: Mary Pfeiffer to Pauline, June 5, 1929, PUL.
"swimming and loafing": Pauline to Virginia, September 16, 1929, *Letters, Vol. 4*, 100.

Jack at the Ranch

the leather quirt: Hemingway, *Misadventures*, 17.
"You know, Schatz": Hemingway, 17.
nearly dying with impatience: Hemingway, 17.
using his pockets: Hemingway, 2.
"were so beautiful": Hemingway, 18.

Biographical Crap

"to at once remove": EH to Maxwell Perkins, July 31, 1930, *Letters, Vol. 4*, 340.
not to answer questions: EH to Grace Hemingway, October 12, 1929, *Letters, Vol. 4*, 120.
"So HeLp Me GoD": EH to Maxwell Perkins, July 31, 1930, *Letters, Vol. 4*, 340.
no copies had yet been: Maxwell Perkins to EH, August 6, 1930, *Letters, Vol. 4*, 343n.

Vive la Marriage

"from the first moment": John Dos Passos, *The Best Times* (New York: The New American Library), 200.

Her Catholic beliefs: Hawkins, *Unbelievable*, 188.

a good trait: EH to Waldo Peirce, *Letters, Vol. 4*, 304.

"Sure we are going": Bill Horne to EH, March 2, 1930, JFK.

The Man Who Invented Montana

"straight legged": Moseley, "Hemingway Remembered."

"on the bum": EH to Milford Baker, August 12, 1930, *Letters, Vol. 4*, 344.

"the river was about": Moseley, "Hemingway Remembered."

"Ernest sat in the sun": Moseley.

The Cow-Eating Bear

"everything but shooting elephants": EH to Henry Strater, June 12, 1930, *Letters, Vol. 4*, 314.

"fear of busting": EH to Archibald MacLeish, August 31, 1930, *Letters, Vol. 4*, 352–353.

The men headed: Chris Warren, *Ernest Hemingway in the Yellowstone High Country* (Helena, MT: Riverbend Publishing, 2019), 45.

Dr. Trueblood: Warren, 45.

for medicinal purposes: Warren, 45.

"Ernest Hemingway was brought": *Cody Enterprise*, August 20, 1930.

Ernest told Ivan stories: Lee Alan Gutkind, "Bearskin Tempting," *Billings Gazette*, October 20, 1970.

"I haven't read": Addison Bragg, "In the Legend," *Billings Gazette*, November 15, 1970.

"If you want": Gutkind, "Bearskin Tempting."

Sparing Goofy: EH to Archibald MacLeish, August 31, 1930, *Letters, Vol. 4*, 352–353.

When he arrived: Gutkind, "Bearskin Tempting."

Big Game Hunter

Plus, he was still: EH to Maxwell Perkins, September 3, 1930, *Letters, Vol. 4*, 354.

"skinning dead horses": EH to Perkins, September 3, 1930, 354.

Girl Friday

"Damn," he said, "I forgot": Lee Gutkind, "Hemingway's Wyoming," *Casper Star Tribune*, October 19, 1970.
"You're dead!": Hemingway, *Misadventures*, 6.

On Stage and Screen

"an awful mess": Milford Baker to EH, September 24, 1930, PUL.

Dos Passos in the High Country

"watching Hem": Dos Passos, *Best Times*, 205.

Admittance Clerk

"Occupation?" she asked: Dan Burkhart, "Hemingway in Billings," *Billings Gazette*, February 22, 1998.

SOS Max

"PLEASE FORWARD": EH to Maxwell Perkins, November 3, 1930, *Letters, Vol. 4*, 395.

Pauline Takes Dictation

more time to practice: EH to Henri Strater, mid-November 1930, *Letters, Vol. 4*, 396.
"Why don't you have Scribner's": EH to Maxwell Perkins, November 17, 1930, *Letters, Vol. 4*, 400.
"It is fine": EH to Perkins, November 17, 1930, 400.

No More Guns

"any former address": EH to Mike Strater, November 23, 1930, *Letters, Vol. 4*, 410.
"faking romanticist": EH to Maxwell Perkins, December 1, 1930, *Letters, Vol. 4*, 416.

A Rotten Time

She encouraged Max: Pauline to Maxwell Perkins, December 1, 1930, *Letters, Vol. 4*, 415.
"The lines": EH to Archibald MacLeish, December 4, 1930, *Letters, Vol. 4*, 420.
"Well. Mac,": EH to MacLeish, December 4, 1930, 420.

Montana in the Rearview Mirror

leaving Montana: PUL, Cable, Western Union destination receipt stamp 1930
DEC 18 PM 12 17.

Part III: 1932

Lovely figure: EH to Guy Hickock, October 14, 1932, *Hemingway Selected Letters,
1917–1961*, ed. Carlos Baker (Great Britain: Panther Books, 1985), 372.

Recovery

bringing her: Michael Reynolds, *Hemingway: The 1930s* (New York: W. W. Norton,
1997), 64.
CHICAGO WOMAN: *Key West Citizen*, March 19, 1931.

The View Ahead

"a certain amount": Hawkins, *Unbelievable*, 141.
"Take good care": EH to Jane and Grant Mason, July 9, 1932, JFK.

Motherhood

"You are the punctuation": Kert, *Hemingway Women*, 233.
Mary Pfeiffer felt Patrick: Mary Pfeiffer to Pauline, June 7, 1932, JFK.

"Hemingway's Death"

"Hemingway's Death": EH to Maxwell Perkins, July 27, 1932, Baker, *Selected
Letters*, 364.
"the regular rule": Maxwell Perkins to EH, July 7, 1932, *The Only Thing That
Counts: The Ernest Hemingway-Maxwell Perkins Correspondence*, ed. Matthew
J. Bruccoli (New York: Simon & Schuster, 1996), 172.2.
If he had included: Form letter EH wrote for Scribner's, undated, Bruccoli, *The
Only Thing*, 179.
Ernest told Max: EH to Maxwell Perkins, June 28, 1932, Baker, *Selected Letters*,
361.

The Five-Year Itch

she flattered Ernest: Hawkins, *Unbelievable*, 140.
"Lovelier than anyone": Pauline to EH, November 30, 1931, JFK.

A Pilgrimage to Powell

Mrs. Hemingway Is: *Key West Citizen*, January 27, 1931.
best shooting: EH to Maxwell Perkins, August 9, 1932, Bruccoli, *The Only Thing*,
176.

No Word

"Poor Old Papa": EH to Jane and Grant Mason, Summer 1932, JFK.

The Murphys

"the man in the silver suit": Honoraria Murphy Donnelly and Richard N. Billings,
Sara & Gerald: Villa America and After (New York: Times Books, 1982), 23.

Honoria in Love

"smooth as a girl's hair": Donnelly and Billings, 66.
so horse crazy: Gerald Murphy to Archibald MacLeish, September 8, 1932, *Letters
from the Lost Generation, Gerald and Sara Murphy and Friends*, ed. Linda
Patterson (New Brunswick, NJ: Rutgers University Press, 1991), 65 (hereafter
Lost Generation Letters).
"the trout would be": Donnelly and Billings, *Sara & Gerald*, 66.
"Don't be afraid": Donnelly and Billings, 67.
no longer afraid: Donnelly and Billings, 67.
"Watch while I": Donnelly and Billings, 67.
"sweet like nectar": Donnelly and Billings, 67.

Perfection

"streams are overflowing": Gerald Murphy to Archibald MacLeish, September 8,
1932, *Lost Generation Letters*, 65.
"for good or bad": Murphy to MacLeish, September 8, 1932, 65.
"My dear boy": Gerald and Sarah Murphy to EH, Miller, fall 1926, *Lost Generation
Letters*, 23–34.
"hardly noticed": Gerald Murphy to Archibald MacLeish, September 8, 1932, *Lost
Generation Letters*, 65.
"approaching perfection": Gerald Murphy to Archibald MacLeish, September 8,
1932, *Lost Generation Letters*, 63.

Woman's Work

"galloping about": Pauline to Maxwell Perkins, September 21, 1932, JFK.

Reviews

Old Bess trembled: Ernest Hemingway, "A Paris Letter," *Esquire*, February 1934.

Disappointment

"obscene" language: Miriam Mandel, *A Companion to Hemingway's Death in the Afternoon* (Rochester, NY: Camden House, 2009), 36.

"style was too dense": Mandel, 36.

"I have never": "Letter to the Editor," *New York Times Book Review*, October 9, 1932.

"better eyes": Kert, *Hemingway Women*, 238.

Charles Shoots a Bear, Ernest Shoots a Bigger Bear

"fraid a nothing": Baker, *A Life Story*, 5.

"killed a hell of a big bear": EH to Henry Strater, October 14, 1932, Baker, *Selected Letters*, 369.

Letters Before Leaving

trout had dropped: Hemingway, "A Paris Letter."

"un-Christly blizzards": EH to Guy Hickok, October 29, 1932, Baker, *Selected Letters*, 375.

Part IV: 1936

After Africa

mosquito netting: Ernest Hemingway, *Green Hills of Africa*, The Hemingway Library Edition (New York: Scribner, 2015), 204.

"flocks of wildebeest": Hemingway, 204.

"drinks, baths": Hemingway, 206.

"felt dreary": Hemingway, 230.

"high and cool": Hemingway, 230.

"Poor little lambs": Hawkins, *Unbelievable*, 164.

"to journey to Africa": Mary Pfeiffer to Pauline, October 31, 1933, PUL.

SITTING DOWN: Guy Hickock, "Sitting Down Is the Best Way to Shoot a Lion," *Brooklyn Daily Eagle*, April 25, 1934.
"four lions": Hawkins, *Unbelievable*, 165.
"The only person": Hemingway, *Green Hills*, 40.
"very desirable": Hemingway, 152.
"and I had no wish": Hemingway, 40.
the greatest writer: Hemingway, 19.
new plaything: Hawkins, *Unbelievable*, 166.

Wyoming After All

the time a gale: Hemingway, *Green Hills*, 60.
"entering the time of life": EH to Sara and Gerald, March 19, 1935, *Lost Generation Letters*, 118.
the only people who really mattered: Reynolds, *The 1930s*, 234.

Changing Course

he missed her: Reynolds, 234.
"a little terrier": Hemingway, *Green Hills*, 45.
"not spoiled": Pauline to EH, June 14, 1935, JFK.

Black Ass Moods

the reviewer was touched: Carl Van Doren, "Hunter's Credo," *Time*, November 4, 1935, 81; Kert, *Hemingway Women*, 273.
"the pursuit and dismemberment": Kert, *Hemingway Women*, 273.
"black ass moods": Hawkins, *Unbelievable*, 183.
"more tolerant": EH to Mary Pfeiffer, January 26, 1936, PUL.

Frenemies

it was a shame: Hemingway, *Green Hills*, 46.
no longer relevant: Hemingway, 47.

The Boys

He didn't come down: Baker, *A Life Story*, 292.

The Rich

"a fairy godfather": Hawkins, *Unbelievable*, 172.
"cook, factotum, and outdoor instructor": Warren, *Yellowstone High Country*, 79.

Tommy Boy

"Aren't you Mr. Hemingway?": Denis Brian, *The True Gen* (New York: Grove Press, 1988), 97.
"Oh shut up": Brian, 100.
"I don't write": Brian, 98.
"Well I'll be goddamned": Brian, 98.

The Elusive Grizzly

"slippery as": EH to Archibald MacLeish, September 26, 1936, Baker, *Selected Letters*, 452–453.
used a trowel: Baker, *A Life Story*, 294.
Ernest lost $900: Baker, 294.

A Change of Seasons

"beautifully in the wind": EH to AM, September 26, 1936, Baker, *Selected Letters*, 452–453.

Hello, Ernest? This Is War Calling . . .

"because he had friends on both sides": Brian, *True Gen*, 103.
without personal bias: Brian, 103.
supported the rebels: Brian, 103.
Arnold cautioned: Baker, *A Life Story*, 300.
"Nothing ever happens": Hawkins, *Unbelievable*, 194.

A Woman Walks into a Bar . . .

"What she felt": Brian, *True Gen*, 102.

Part V: 1938–1939

An excellent editor: EH to Maxwell Perkins, ca. January 14, 1940, in Bruccoli, *The Only Thing*, 277.

A Hero's Welcome

"life here": Pauline to EH, April 29, 1938, JFK.
"Ernest seems": Pauline and EH to Paul and Mary Pfeiffer, June 11–13, 1938, PUL.
Pauline realized: Hawkins, *Unbelievable*, 203.
"pack Papa's western gear": Reynolds, *The 1930s*, 293.

Home, Somewhat Sweet Home

"Am going home": EH to Mike and Helen Ward, May 26, 1938, JFK.
tremendous jam: Baker, *A Life Story*, 335.
had suggested marriage: Kert, *Hemingway Women*, 316.
Ernest accused her: Hawkins, *Unbelievable*, 196.

No Holding Back

he blamed her: Hawkins, *Unbelievable*, 210.

A Cause for Concern?

"But they aren't built": Ernest Hemingway, *To Have and Have Not* (New York: Scribner, 2003), 244–245.

Hitler Threatens

"To Marty and Herbert": Baker, *A Life Story*, 333.
he promised her: Reynolds, *The 1930s*, 294.

Time with the Boys

"But I do hope": Pauline to EH, September 2, 1938, JFK.
"fine solid way": Pauline to EH, September 6, 1938, JFK.
"My you are a lovely": Pauline to EH, September 6, 1938, JFK.
"she does not hear": Pauline to EH, September 17, 1938, JFK.

Paris

"Perhaps my dear fellow": Pauline to EH, October 18, 1938, JFK.

Havana Nights

As Ernest hung up: Hawkins, *Unbelievable*, 218.

Struck by Lightning

"would be quite simple": Pauline to EH, July 8, 1939, JFK.
"Relax and enjoy": Pauline to EH, July 9, 1939, JFK.
"Dearest Papa": Pauline to EH, July 9, 1939, JFK.

The Real Reason

"prettier all the time": EH to Thomas Shevlin, April 4, 1939, Baker, *Selected Letters*, 483.

The Reunion

he had wished: Ernest Hemingway, *A Moveable Feast*, the Restored Edition (New York: Scribner, 2009), 218.

Hope in a Letter

"renewing my youth": Pauline to EH, August 5–7, 1939, JFK.
"trying to give you an idea": Pauline to EH, August 5–7, 1939, JFK.
"DO have a good time": Pauline to EH, August 5–7, 1939, JFK.

Talking with Bears

"to talk to two bears": Hemingway, *Misadventure*s, 35.
"Hey, Bear": Hemingway, 35.
"Bear, you dumb": Hemingway, 35.
"figure of authority": Hemingway, 36.

War

light of a kerosene lamp: Warren, *Yellowstone High Country*, 106.
"The Germans have marched": Warren, 107.
drove across the meadow: Warren, 107.

Casualties

"Oh Papa, darling": PH to EH, August 11, 1939, JFK.
when he made up his mind: Hawkins, *Unbelievable*, 224.

When He Came Up for Air

Pauline wrote to him: EH to Hadley Mowrer, November 24, 1939, Baker, *Selected Letters*, 496.
what Jack's Christmas: EH to Mowrer, November 24, 1939, 496.
welcome to join: Baker, *A Life Story*, 344.

Epilogue: 1940

"Bravest woman": Kert, *Hemingway Women*, 299.

"Would never be": Hawkins, *Unbelievable*, 225.

Paid her own way: Kert, *Hemingway Women*, 326.

Friends with Eleanor Roosevelt: EH to Mary Pfeiffer, August 2, 1937, Baker, *Selected Letters*, 459–460.

Could maybe produce: Baker, *A Life Story*, 355.

"so damned happy": Kert, *Hemingway Women*, 342.

Success

"Hemingway the artist": Edmund Wilson, "Return of Ernest Hemingway" (Review of *For Whom the Bell Tolls*), *New Republic* CIII, October 28, 1940.

"Those who live": Kert, *Hemingway Women*, 422.

"You never had it": Ernest Hemingway, *For Whom the Bell Tolls* (New York: Charles Scribner's Sons, 1940), 315.

"pretty to think so": Ernest Hemingway, *The Sun Also Rises* (New York: Scribner, 2006), 220.

BIBLIOGRAPHY

Adams, J. Donald. "Ernest Hemingway's First Novel in Eight Years." *New York Times*, October 17, 1937.

Baker, Allie. "Hadley Talks About the Lost Manuscripts." The Hemingway Project. April 18, 2013. https://www.thehemingwayproject.com/2018/08 /22/hadley-talks-about-the-lost-manuscripts/.

Baker, Carlos. *Ernest Hemingway: A Life Story*. New York: Charles Scribner's Sons, 1969.

Baker, Carlos, ed. *Ernest Hemingway: Selected Letters, 1917–1961*. New York: Charles Scribner's Sons, 1981.

Baker, Carlos. *Hemingway: The Writer as Artist*. Princeton: Princeton University Press, 1972.

Blume, Lesley M. M. *Everybody Behaves Badly: The True Story Behind Hemingway's Masterpiece* The Sun Also Rises. Boston: Houghton Mifflin Harcourt Publishing, 2016.

Boyle, Kay, and Robert McAlmon. *Being Geniuses Together: A Binocular View of Paris in the '20s*. New York: Doubleday & Co., 1968.

Bragg, Addison. "In the Legend." *Billings Gazette*, November 15, 1970.

Brian, Denis. *The True Gen*. New York: Grove Press, 1988.

Bruccoli, Matthew J., ed. *The Only Thing That Counts: The Ernest Hemingway–Maxwell Perkins Correspondence*. New York: Scribner, 1996.

Bruccoli, Matthew J., and Margaret M. Duggan, eds. *Correspondence of F. Scott Fitzgerald*. New York: Random House, 1980.

Burgess, Anthony. *Ernest Hemingway and His World*. New York: Charles Scribner's Sons, 1978.

Burkhart, Dan. "Hemingway in Billings." *Billings Gazette*, February 22, 1998.

Callaghan, Morley. *That Summer in Paris*. New York: Coward-McCann, 1963.

Cannell, Kathleen. "Scenes with a Hero." In *Hemingway and the Sun Set*, edited by Bertram D. Sarason, 145–147. Washington, DC: NCR, Microcard Editions, 1972.

Carpenter, Humphrey. *Geniuses Together: American Writers in Paris in the 1920s*. Boston: Houghton Mifflin Company, 1988.

Carr, Virginia Spencer. *Dos Passos: A Life*. New York: Doubleday & Co.,1984.

Clark, Edwin. "Scott Fitzgerald Looks into Middle Age." *New York Times*, April 19, 1925.

Daugherty, John. *A Place Called Jackson Hole*. Moose, WY: Grand Teton National Park Service, 1999.

Diliberto, Gioia. *Paris Without End: The True Story of Hemingway's First Wife*. New York: Harper Perennial, 2011.

Donnelly, Honoria Murphy, and Richard N. Billings. *Sara & Gerald: Villa America and After*. New York: Times Books, 1982.

Dos Passos, John. *The Best Times: An Informal Memoir*. New York: New American Library, 1966.

———. *The Fourteenth Chronicle: Letters and Diaries of John Dos Passos*. Edited by Townsend Ludington. Boston: Gambit, 1973.

Fitch, Noël Riley. *Literary Cafés of Paris*. Montgomery: Starrhill Press, 1989.

———. *Sylvia Beach and the Lost Generation*. New York: W. W. Norton, 1985.

———. *The Letters of F. Scott Fitzgerald*. Edited by Robert Turnbull. New York: Charles Scribner's Sons, 1963.

Fitzgerald, F. Scott. "The Crack-Up." *Esquire*, February 1936, 41.

Galantiere, Lewis. "There Is Never Any End to Paris." *New York Times*, May 10, 1964.

Griffin, Peter. *Less Than a Treason: Hemingway in Paris*. New York: Oxford University Press, 1990.

Gutkind, Lee Alan. "Bearskin Tempting." *Billings Gazette*, October 20, 1970.

———. "Fishing, Writing, Drinking." *Billings Gazette*, October 25, 1970.

———. "Sheridan Couple Put In Story." *Billings Gazette*, October 18, 1970.

Hawkins, Ruth A. *Unbelievable Happiness and Final Sorrow: The Hemingway-Pfeiffer Marriage*. Fayetteville, AR: University of Arkansas Press, 2012.

Hemingway, Ernest. "The Art of Fiction XXI." Interview. *Paris Review*, Spring 1958.

———. "The Art of the Short Story." *Paris Review*, Spring 1981.

———. *The Complete Short Stories of Ernest Hemingway*. The Finco Vigia edition. New York: Charles Scribner's Sons, 1987.

———. *Death in the Afternoon.* New York: Charles Scribner's Sons, 1932.

———. *A Farewell to Arms.* New York: Charles Scribner's Sons, 1929.

———. *A Farewell to Arms.* The Hemingway Library edition. New York: Scribner, 2012.

———. *The Fifth Column and Four Stories of the Spanish Civil War.* London: Arrow Books, 2013.

———. *For Whom the Bell Tolls.* The Hemingway Library edition. New York: Scribner, 2019.

———. *For Whom the Bell Tolls.* New York: Charles Scribner's Sons, 1940.

———. *Green Hills of Africa.* New York: Scribner, 2003.

———. *Green Hills of Africa.* The Hemingway Library edition. New York: Scribner, 2015.

———. *In Our Time.* New York: Scribner Paperback Fiction, 1996.

———. *Men Without Women.* New York: Charles Scribner's Sons, 1927.

———. *A Moveable Feast.* New York: Charles Scribner's Sons, 1964.

———. *A Moveable Feast.* The Restored Edition. New York: Scribner, 2009.

———. "A Paris Letter." *Esquire,* February 1934.

———. *The Short Stories of Ernest Hemingway.* The Modern Library edition. New York: Random House, 1938.

———. "The Sights of Whitehead Street: A Key West Letter." *Esquire,* April 1935.

———. *The Sun Also Rises.* New York: Scribner, 2006.

———. *The Sun Also Rises.* The Hemingway Library edition. New York: Scribner, 2014.

———. *To Have and Have Not.* New York: Scribner, 2003.

———. *Winner Take Nothing.* New York: Scribner's Sons, 1970.

Hemingway, Jack. *Misadventures of a Fly Fisherman: My Life with and Without Papa.* Dallas, TX: Taylor Publishing Co., 1986.

Hemingway, Valerie. *Running with the Bulls: My Years with the Hemingways.* New York: Ballantine, 2005.

Hendrickson, Paul. *Hemingway's Boat: Everything He Loved in Life, and Lost.* New York: Vintage Books, 2012.

Hotchner, A. E. "Don't Touch 'A Moveable Feast.'" *New York Times,* July 19, 2009.

———. *Hemingway in Love, His Own Story.* New York: Saint Martin's Press, 2015.

———. *Papa Hemingway: A Personal Memoir.* New York: Random House, 1966.

Hutchinson, Percy. "Mr. Hemingway Shows Himself Master Craftsman in the Short Story." *New York Times*, October 16, 1927.

Kert, Bernice. *The Hemingway Women: Those Who Loved Him—The Wives and Others*. New York: W. W. Norton, 1986.

Loeb, Harold. *The Way It Was*. New York: Criterion Books, 1959.

Lynn, Kenneth S. *Hemingway*. Cambridge, MA: Harvard University Press, 1987.

Mandel, Miriam. *A Companion to Hemingway's Death in the Afternoon*. Rochester, NY: Camden House, 2004.

Mellow, James L. *Hemingway: A Life Without Consequences*. London: Hodder & Stoughton, 1993.

Meyers, Jeffery. *Hemingway: A Biography*. New York: Da Capo Press, 1985.

Moorehead, Caroline. *Selected Letters of Martha Gellhorn*. New York: Henry Holt and Co., 2006.

Moseley, Virginia K. "Hemingway Remembered." *Barrington Courier Review*, September 27, 1979.

Patterson, Miller. *Letters from the Lost Generation, Gerald and Sara Murphy and Friends*. New Brunswick, NJ: Rutgers University Press, 1946.

Paul, Steve. *Hemingway at Eighteen: The Pivotal Year That Launched an American Legend*. Chicago: Chicago Review Press, 2018.

Reynolds, Michael. *Hemingway: The Paris Years*. New York: W. W. Norton, 1999.

———. *Hemingway: The 1930s*. New York: W. W. Norton, 1997.

Sarason, Bertram D. *Hemingway and the Sun Set*. Washington, DC: National Cash Register Company, 1972.

Sindelar, Nancy. *Influencing Hemingway: People and Places That Shaped His Life and Work*. Lanham, MD: Rowman & Littlefield, 2014.

Slack, Judy. *Ernest Hemingway: His 1928 Stay in the Bighorn Mountains of Wyoming*. Sheridan, WY: The Wyoming Room, Sheridan County Fulmer Public Library, 2011.

Spanier, Sandra, Albert J. Defazio III, and Robert W. Trogdon, eds. *The Letters of Ernest Hemingway, Vol. 2: 1923–1925*. Cambridge: Cambridge University Press, 2013.

Spanier, Sandra, Rena Sanderson, and Robert W. Trogdon, eds. *The Letters of Ernest Hemingway, Vol. 3: 1926–1929*. Cambridge: Cambridge University Press, 2015.

Spanier, Sandra, and Miriam Mandel, eds. *The Letters of Ernest Hemingway, Vol. 4: 1929–1931*. Cambridge: Cambridge University Press, 2018.

Stein, Gertrude. *The Autobiography of Alice B. Toklas*. London: Penguin Books, 1966.

Warren, Christopher. *Ernest Hemingway in the Yellowstone High Country*. Helena, MT: Riverbend Publishing, 2019.

White, William, ed. *By-Line Ernest Hemingway: Selected Articles and Dispatches of Four Decades*. New York: Charles Scribner's Sons, 1967.

Wilson, Edmund. "Return of Ernest Hemingway." *New Republic*, CIII, October 28, 1940.

INDEX